TENDING YOUR GARDEN

ALSO BY GORDON AND MARY HAYWARD

The Intimate Garden:
Twenty Years and Four Seasons in Our Garden

ALSO BY GORDON HAYWARD

Stone in the Garden

Your House, Your Garden

The Welcoming Garden

Tending Your Garden

A YEAR-ROUND GUIDE TO GARDEN MAINTENANCE

GORDON AND MARY HAYWARD

PHOTOGRAPHS BY
RICHARD W. BROWN

W. W. NORTON & COMPANY

NEW YORK ■ LONDON

For information about permission to reproduce selections from this book, write to
Permissions, W. W. Norton & Company, Inc., 500 Fifth Avenue, New York, NY 10110

Manufacturing by RR Donnelley, Roanoke
Book design by Marilyn Appleby Design
Production manager: Andrew Marasia

Library of Congress Cataloging-in-Publication Data

Hayward, Gordon.
Tending your garden : a year-round guide to garden maintenance /
Gordon and Mary Hayward ; photographs by Richard W. Brown. — 1st ed.
p. cm.
Includes bibliographical references and index.
ISBN-13: 978-0-393-05904-5 (hardcover)
ISBN-10: 0-393-05904-9 (hardcover)
1. Gardening. 2. Gardens. I. Hayward, Mary. II. Title.
SB453.H345 2007
635.9—dc22
2006023334

W. W. Norton & Company, Inc., 500 Fifth Avenue, New York, N.Y. 10110
www.wwnorton.com

W. W. Norton & Company Ltd., Castle House, 75/76 Wells Street, London W1T 3QT

1 2 3 4 5 6 7 8 9 0

*We dedicate this book to
Richard Brown, photographer.*

Figure 1. June in front of the garden shed.

IL FAUT CULTIVER NOTRE JARDIN.

(IT IS NECESSARY TO CULTIVATE OUR GARDEN.)

—VOLTAIRE, *CANDIDE*

Contents

INTRODUCTION • 11

■ **WINTER • 21**
INTRODUCTION • 21
PRUNING DECIDUOUS TREES • 25
PRUNING VINES AND SHRUBS • 35
CHECKLISTS: LATE AUTUMN/EARLY WINTER, LATE
WINTER • 50

■ **SPRING • 53**
INTRODUCTION • 53
CLEANUP • 59
PLANTING TREES AND SHRUBS • 71
PLANTING PERENNIALS AND ANNUALS • 92
CHECKLISTS: EARLY SPRING, LATE SPRING • 107

■ **SUMMER • 113**
INTRODUCTION • 113
BED MAINTENANCE • 117
DEADHEADING PERENNIALS • 125
REMOVING INVASIVE PLANTS • 139
HEDGE TRIMMING • 147
CHECKLISTS: JUNE INTO JULY,
JULY INTO AUGUST • 149

■ **AUTUMN • 155**
INTRODUCTION • 155
CUTTING BACK PERENNIALS • 157
DIVIDING PLANTS • 169
PLANTING BULBS • 179
LEAF MANAGEMENT • 189
REPAIRING A BREAK IN A DRY STONE WALL • 198
CHECKLIST: AUTUMN • 204

APPENDIX • 215
BIBLIOGRAPHY • 223
INDEX • 231

Acknowledgments

FIRST AND FOREMOST, WE WOULD LIKE TO THANK Richard Brown, a Vermont-based photographer, for his clear, honest and beautiful pictures taken not with a digital camera but with an old 35-mm Nikon. Richard photographed our garden six times during the 2005 growing season for this book, and seven times in 2003 for our preceding book, *The Intimate Garden*. Richard combines his keen eye for composition with his take on what he photographs to create approachable, honest, and revealing images.

We also want to thank all the people who have helped us with our garden over the years, especially Robin Garlick, Siena MacFarland, and Patricia Sanzone, who have been with us every Wednesday during the growing season for the past five years. Their considerable skills, good humor, and dedication to the work has made all the difference.

We also want to thank Torben Larsen of Windham Growers and his crew of hard working men for all their help over the years in our garden along with the installation of the many, many gardens I have designed for clients in our area of New England.

Finally, we would like to thank our son Nate for teaching us by his fine and principled example how to live lightly on the land and how to keep that land in good heart. We have learned so very much from you, Nate. Thank you.

Introduction

Figure I-1. *Begonia* × *tuberhybrida* 'Illumination Apricot' bloomed like this nonstop from the day we planted it until early October. **Figure I-2.** (Opposite) All the work that we put in to maintaining our 1½ acres of gardens comes to fruition when we can look out of our windows, or back at the house, and feel that our house is *in* a garden.

MAINTENANCE *IS* GARDENING. Maintenance encompasses all those caring, creative acts centered around pruning and edging, dividing and transplanting, deadheading and weeding, cutting back and composting. You put plants in the ground, then look after them; you observe plants closely and measure time by their growth. In protecting them from severe weather, pests, diseases, and weeds—as well as observing the inevitable changes that mark their growth, maturity, and decay—you are simultaneously looking after the design you set them into.

If you attend to maintenance in a conscious, caring, and efficient way, the rewards are indeed deep. Modern technological life separates us from the natural world; the work of the garden reconnects us to the natural world of sun and shade, rain and mist, and the slow passage of time. Garden maintenance, which is all about fostering balance in a garden and its design, teaches us about change, about adapting, about seeing loss as a springboard for possibility. Garden maintenance has certainly taught us humility in this complex pursuit.

Maintenance is necessary and hugely satisfying work, in part because you become nature's ally. And there's no getting around *the work*. The willingness to put effort into your garden is at the heart of what it is to be a gardener. You know plenty about what it feels like when you put work into your garden in April and May, then let things slide a bit in June. Before you know it, the garden is a patch of weeds and you're either in denial or disappointed. It doesn't have to be that way if you plant wisely, start small, and build your confidence.

Although there are times during the seven-month growing season here in Vermont when we feel overwhelmed by the work, above all we feel pleasure and renewal in the weeding, raking, planting, pruning, mowing, and the many other jobs this book describes. After mowing the lawn myself, I look back with pleasure at how good the place looks. When pruning our apple trees, I feel connected to my childhood growing up on an orchard in northwestern Connecticut. When my wife, Mary, weeds meticulously, she is living out skills that her mother showed her growing up on a farm in the Cotswold Hills of England. She also finds it to be a form of meditation, where her body is so deeply involved in tasks that her mind can wander free. She loses a sense of time when she weeds mindfully. This is not an intellectual pursuit but a physical one; your awareness is heightened. You notice the smallest changes in the garden, and seeing them changes you.

Mary and I grew up on working farms. These were no gentleman farms with hired help. We hold a sound work ethic within us because of our childhood experiences, which are unusual today. Yet we do not want to overwhelm you with the fact that we look after an intensively planted acre and a half of organic garden. You may not have or want that much garden. What we want to do in this book is share what we have learned so you can take new pleasure in the work of gardening. That pleasure rests on knowledge, on confidence that you are gardening well.

We started developing this garden in southern Vermont in 1983. Although we had a bit of help for the first eighteen years, Mary and I expanded and maintained the garden pretty much on our own. Then, shortly before we both turned sixty, we hired three ladies to help us one day a week from mid-April until the leaves were all raked up in late October. Every Wednesday, Siena MacFarland, Patricia Sanzone, and Robin Garlick arrive for the day. Since we have worked together, they have been developing gardens of their own (even though each of them rents an apartment). They say they can't *not* garden. They have been of inestimable help to us.

Although Mary and I work 30 hours or more a week beyond the 24 hours a week that Siena, Patricia, and Robin work, we don't want to hold you to that schedule. Our object is not to exhaust you. The point is that, yes, gardening is work. But you can choose how much time you want to put into your garden by the way you design it, by how big or small you make it, by the types of plants you choose, and by the degree to which you attend to detail. Your garden need not

Figure I-3. It took twenty-five years of steady work and thoughtful maintenance to get our garden to look like this. Don't be overwhelmed by our obsession; learn from it and make your own garden your own way.

Figure I-4. It takes time to fill the birdbath and float peonies in it, but visual moments such as this make all the difference. Beauty lies in details.

look like ours or be as big as ours. You may not want to live and breathe gardening the way we do. And that's just fine.

LEARN BY DOING

This book provides you with a season-by-season guide to the primary work of any garden in North America. We hope this book helps you see the overall picture of what it takes to look after a garden. Then, with that knowledge, you can proceed with confidence.

Although Mary and I grew up on farms, that doesn't mean we grew up gardening. Sure, we learned a bit here and a bit there. But we have really taught ourselves. We've learned by trial and error, by reading, by experimenting, by visiting gardens and talking with gardeners about how they do this and how they do that. We've written this book so that you can get where we are now in our gardening lives a lot faster than we did.

This book is a record of what we have learned over twenty-five years. It may contain far more than you want to know about the subject, so we have arranged information so you can look in the index or the contents to rapidly find answers to many questions about working in your garden: how to handle the edge where bed meets lawn; how to prune a crab apple; how to deadhead perennials; how to lay stone.

Although you may not live in Zone 4, or even in Vermont, there is no end of information herein that will apply wherever you live, whatever size your garden might be. Keep your own garden in mind as you read, then put that information to work in your own garden. Learn from this book; don't be driven by it.

KNOWLEDGE LEADS TO CONFIDENCE

A lot of people across America are not gardening, or gardening far more modestly than they would like to, because they fear they may not be doing everything right. Gardening is a public act in many ways. When you launch into making a garden, you're putting your creativity out there for guests and family and neighbors to see, and—you fear—judge. There's a certain vulnerability in the act of gardening. It's like the feeling you had in seventh grade when your English teacher asked you to read your essay out loud to the whole class and you were mortified. Yet you did read it, and probably everyone in the class admired you for it. Will and Sara Anne Godwin, from Hagerstown, Maryland, put a small garden in front of their house, one I helped lay out, and now gardens between sidewalk and front door are popping up all over their neighborhood. Maybe they're not all "perfect." They don't have to be (unless you are a driven perfectionist). Your garden can look the way you want it to look. If there are a few weeds, so be it. Call it your Romantic Garden.

MAINTENANCE UNDERPINS STYLE, TONE, DESIGN

Maintaining a garden is striking a balance between the look of the garden you're comfortable with and its health. Every job you do, whether raking leaves, weeding dandelions, or pruning a magnolia, has implications for the design and health of the garden. When we edge a lawn path, for example, the garden looks much better—the design is clarified—but we've also prevented grass from competing with perennials at the edge of a bed, thereby increasing the health and well-being of the garden.

The look you want for your healthy garden results from a combination of its design and maintenance. And that look has a lot to do with how your garden makes people feel. I hope this book will help you find your maintenance style, because to a large degree the nature of the work you do in your garden affects its tone and mood. For example, we want our garden in Vermont to feel relaxed and approachable, and not draw undue attention to itself. We don't want to pull off a tour de force of design or maintenance; we want people to feel comfortable here.

We once saw the antithesis of our desired garden. We walked into a mixed border and were struck not by the beauty of the garden but by the fact that there were hundreds of beige bamboo stakes holding up dahlias, hollyhocks, and all manner of perennials and annuals. It was a tour de force of staking. It was an approach to garden maintenance that drew attention to itself, thereby lifting that area out of the otherwise coherent broader garden. We certainly don't want our 7-foot-high blooms of *Crambe cordifolia* flopping onto their neighbors, so we stake, but in such a way that the stems and leaves hide the stakes, allowing the plant to be itself.

The way we maintain our garden harmonizes with its design. We garden on old farmland around a 200-year-old farmhouse. Views look out on the practical beauty of hayfields. If you look over our preceding book, *The Intimate Garden*, you'll see what I mean. We live a rural life, so to go into our garden and stake and tie up and edge to absolute perfection every few weeks would be inconsistent with the easy feel the place calls for. The maintenance style we're after is one that is appropriate for *our* garden. We want the beauty of the garden to slowly reveal itself, not overwhelm with our extraordinary design or maintenance skills.

MAINTENANCE IS MANAGEMENT

We learned a valuable maintenance lesson from our friend John Sales, who was in charge of all the gardens for the National Trust in England for many years. He looks at garden maintenance as management. Maintenance is about knowing the when and why of doing all the jobs that keep a garden in good heart and balance.

Years ago we wanted spring-blooming woodland phlox (*Phlox divaricata*) to spread in our Woodland Garden, but we didn't want to spend a lot of money buying lots of plants. Instead we managed the Woodland Garden wisely. We waited for the seeds of the eighteen plants we did buy to mature before string-trimming the spent flower

Figure I-5. The hundred-year-old tool shed that was here when we bought the place in 1983 is action central for maintenance work. All gardeners need a shed or a place to keep tools (and themselves) organized and efficient.

ONE STEP AT A TIME

If you feel overwhelmed by the work required to maintain your garden, read Anne Lamott's book *Bird by Bird: Some Instructions on Writing and Life* (Pantheon Books, 1994). The central metaphor of the book is the story she tells about her ten-year-old brother coming home from school one day. He was agonizing over the fact that he had to write a lengthy paper about birds. Their father encouraged him by saying, "Just take it bird by bird." Look at garden maintenance in the same way—as a series of small steps that add up to big changes.

heads (see Figure AU-19 on page 166). In timing the job this way, the act of trimming the spent flower heads spread seed across the soil of the Woodland Garden, and now a blanket of woodland phlox blooms every spring over a broad area. On the other hand, we are quick to deadhead *Allium aflatunense* the moment the flowers begin to look unsightly. By managing *Allium aflatunense* in this way, we prevent the setting and distribution of seed, thereby avoiding having to weed out thousands of seedlings the following spring.

Maintenance, then, is the overall effort of keeping up the garden so as to manage and direct the flow of change inherent in growth, decline, and decay. Maintenance is so much broader than weeding. Planting is creative; maintenance is sustaining and creative. Having said that, maintenance is not romantic; it is often demanding, repetitive work. But if you give yourself to it, the act will reward you many times over. At the end of the day, when you've cleaned up, settled down, and walk refreshed back into the garden to admire the results of your labor, there is nothing quite like the satisfaction of seeing work well done.

JACKY WARD

In maintaining your garden, you link yourself with countless people worldwide who have looked after gardens over the centuries and continue to do so.

In July 2001, Mary and I led a small group of ladies from the Eastern Shore of Maryland to look at gardens in Ireland. One Sunday afternoon we drove from Kenmare west down the Kenmare River, County Kerry, toward Lauragh. We were on our way to see Derreen, a garden started in the late 1600s and still owned by the same family. It is owned today by Mr. and Mrs. David Bigham, son of Viscountess Mersey, granddaughter of the fifth Marquess of Landsdowne. We met none of these people. We met Jacky Ward, the gardener.

Jacky, who was in his late fifties when we met, grew up at Derreen and worked as a boy next to his father, who was in charge of maintaining the many acres of gardens. Jacky took over that role decades ago. As we walked the garden on paths with names such as Boathouse Walk, Little Oozy, and Glade Walk, we peeked through openings in dense shelter-belt plantings to Kilmakilloge Harbour and the Kenmare River beyond. We took Goleen Walk with Jacky and ended up at Knockatee Seat, from which we could see the mountain of that name in the background and cormorants, guillemots, and herons in the inlets. And as we walked through The King's Oozy, we found ourselves in a semi-tropical world of enormous tree ferns growing at the edges of drainage canals that Jacky or his father had dug. These tree ferns were in turn growing under the protection of vast 300-year-old oaks. Jacky had been working for weeks in this area, pruning, removing undergrowth, and opening views deep into mature forest so he could start replanting ground covers and shade-loving perennials.

As we stood in The King's Oozy listening to Jacky, I realized that the distinction was very unclear between this man and the tree ferns and oaks, the sea and the sky, the mountains beyond and earth below. Jacky Ward was utterly of this place. He knew that when the sky held cumulus clouds, fair weather was ahead, but that mare's tails meant a storm was approaching. His bones told him when it was going to rain. He'd been to Dublin only once, but he knew this place, and was one with it.

Figure W-1. (Opposite) The crisp shapes of yew (*Taxus* × *media* 'Hicksii') and *Viburnum prunifolium* hedges result from trimming in mid-August. These shorn hedges provide the backbone of the winter garden.

Winter

Figure W-2. (Opposite) Pruning the weeping pea shrubs (*Caragana arborescens* 'Pendula') and shearing the low Korean boxwood hedges (*Buxus microphylla koreana*) and the arborvitae hedge (*Thuja occidentalis* 'Smaragd') in the four-quadrant herb garden makes the garden look good twelve months of the year. **Figure W-3.** I simply can't work in the garden without the right gloves. These supple yet strong Afghani goatskin gloves are made by Kurt Haupt and his son at their eighty-year-old Green Mountain Glove Company, in Randolph, Vermont.

IN FEBRUARY 1987, I ATTENDED A GARDEN DESIGN symposium in Boston. People from across America had come to learn from the experts. Near the end of the day, when it was time for the Q&A, a woman from California asked the speaker from New England, "What's it like not to be able to garden twelve months of the year?" Before the speaker could answer the question, those of us from New England, as if in a chorus, called out, "It's wonderful!" If it weren't for winter, I would never have had time to write this book or the others before it. Winter is a gift of time to gardeners.

Winter is when at least those of us in the northern reaches of North America get to step back from the garden for three to five or more months to take stock. Sometimes this means thinking about everything but the garden. But then, if you're reading this book in winter (and I'm writing this book in winter), you know as well as I do that our gardens are never far from our thoughts.

One of the principles I have been arguing for years as a lecturer, writer, and designer is that we need to design our gardens so that when we look out of important windows or open key doors even in winter, we see beauty. We see the gates and sculpture, the framework and structure that we have left in the garden for the winter. And we also see the results of our careful work as well as work yet to be done.

Just this morning 12 inches of light, fluffy snow fell on southern Vermont and on our garden. One of the first things I did when the snow stopped was to go out with a broom and beat the snow free from the laden branches of evergreens: arborvitae (*Thuja occidentalis*), dwarf Scots pine (*Pinus sylvestris* 'Nana'), false cypress (*Chamaecyparis pisifera* 'Filifera'). If I hadn't done so, some of the more brittle branches might have snapped under the weight of the snow.

When I look down sight lines from the key windows and doors of our old house, I see the twelve-tree crab apple orchard in the garden, and behind it the huge old standard McIntosh apple tree, which I have been pruning for twenty-seven years. In February or early March, I'll look out those key windows and those trees will be there, just as they are now, ready for pruning. It will be the pleasure of work—son of a Connecticut orchardist that I am—that will draw me to those trees as surely as the snow will melt. I know after a winter's tea and scones, after reflecting on the garden's design and purpose and development, after placing the plant orders and making sketches, that the moment I can, I'll be in the garden working.

Having said that, every autumn we breathe a

SHARPENING TOOLS

Every late winter, I take time to sharpen all my tools with blades using a diamond dust file: pruning shears, lopping shears, hedge shears, and my axe. The best way to hold them for sharpening is with a vice. I sharpen my pruning shears nearly every time before I prune woody plants. Every year or so, I also take hoes, shovels, and other edged tools that I need to drive into soil to someone who can sharpen them with a motorized grinding wheel.

The result of all this sharpening is twofold. First, work is eased. It takes a lot less effort to hoe or shovel with a sharp blade because it slides through soil with greater ease than would a dull one. Second, because sharpness means less force to hoe, shovel, or cut, a sharp blade is a safer blade. That may sound like a contradiction, but it's true. Sharp blades on all my tools means that they are working as they are meant to work. I don't have to use force to cut through the top growth or roots of a stubborn woody-stemmed weed.

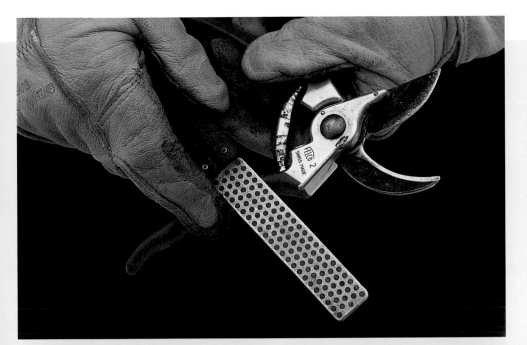

Figure W-4. I use a diamond dust file to sharpen small-bladed hand tools. Each of the little black dots on this tool is embedded with diamond dust. After use, I swing the two-part handle back over the business end of this file to protect it.

Figure W-5. I use Felco #2 pruning shears, because they are just right for the size of my hand. Mary uses the smaller #6s. Sharpen only the beveled side of the blade; leave the flat back side as is. (As you can see, I hold the file at the same angle as that of the sharpened blade as it came from the factory.) I always use bypass rather than anvil shears. With anvil shears, the plant stem rests on a flat surface and the blade passes through the stem, then stops when it comes in contact with the anvil. The stem is crushed in the process. With bypass shears, the blade slices through a stem, then passes by the lower anvil blade; this action doesn't crush the stem.

Figure W-6. A sharp blade on lopping shears, or any shears for that matter, means that you don't have to force the blade through roots or branches. A sharp blade means that you're safer and you don't strain your muscles or tool handles. The cut is also cleaner and heals more rapidly.

Figure W-7. By shearing the four boxwoods in August, by leaving several clumps of the dramatic ornamental grass *Miscanthus sinensis* 'Purpurascens' when we cut back perennials in October, and by leaving the outdoor furniture under the cover of the gazebo, we are able to keep the Long Borders looking good even through the winter.

sigh of relief that the work is finished. The outdoor furniture is stored in the barn, the pots are planted with tulips and stored in the cold part of the cellar, the leaves are raked and perennials cut back, and we relax to enjoy the winter. But the moment we can see dirt, and I mean just a few square feet of it, we're back at it. I don't waste a minute in late winter and very early spring, because I know how much there is to do in spring. As soon the receding snow reveals a patch of lawn, I am on it with a lawn rake. We pick up sticks blown from the cherry trees and maples, the ash trees and black locusts. I don't wait a day

longer than is necessary, because I know that if I don't stay on top of this multitude of spring jobs, I'll get behind and the work will become burdensome.

Yet we have to restrain ourselves. Patches of garden soil appear as the snow retreats, but we're cautious about starting any work on it until the subsurface has thawed and the topsoil has had a chance to dry out a bit. Stepping onto wet soil compacts it, and compaction prevents an easy root run for perennials that aim to send their feeder roots into the soil for sustenance.

Pruning Deciduous Trees

CUTTING BRANCHES FROM TREES

Sometimes it's necessary to cut the lower branches from trees to allow more sunlight to reach the plants growing under the tree, or to make a path more accessible. As shown in the photographs below, I wanted to remove this particular branch from a yellowwood tree to get more direct sunlight to the arborvitae hedge seen in the background in Figure W-8. When making a smaller cut such as this, I turn to a sharp pruning saw such as the one seen in these photographs. To cut off a branch, I follow a sequence of tasks.

Figure W-8. The first step reduces the weight of the branch; I simply saw through the branch at a point about 2 feet out from the trunk. By removing most of the weight of the branch in this simple way, I gain greater control over what remains, and reduce the risk of an accident.

Figure W-9. The second step is to make an upward cut at the bottom of what is known as the collar of a branch. (Look closely at Figure W-11 and you'll see that the collar is not absolutely flush with the trunk but stands just a bit out from it.) I make this cut to prevent tearing the bark when making the final cut.

Figure W-10. The third step is to make the final cut from above. When you make the final stroke with the saw, you will be flush with the cut that you made in Figure W-9.

Figure W-11. The result is a clean cut that the tree will enclose with new bark over the course of three to four years. Notice that I have not covered the exposed wood with the black sealing compound that has been used for many years. The use of that product has been proven to impede healing.

Figure W-12. (Opposite) I took three years to restore this long-neglected tree. The first year I pruned out deadwood and shaded interior branches. The second year I cut back vertical leaders back by two-thirds. The third year I thinned out exterior branches to let sunlight into the tree.

PRUNING APPLE TREES FOR LOOKS AND FRUIT

Pruning is practical and aesthetic, especially in a garden setting. Although I prune crab apple and standard apple trees for flowers and fruit, I am equally aware of how I am shaping the trees. As I prune the interior of our crab apples and the big standard apple in our garden, I pay attention to the lines and forms of the branches and how the removal of interior branches will help show the beautiful interplay of trunk, branch, and twig. I do this work in the dead of winter when the tree is dormant and the sap is not running. In southern Vermont, that means January or February.

Here's the sequence I follow when pruning apple trees—first the big McIntosh tree that was on the property when we bought it years ago; second an ornamental crab apple tree.

Figure W-13. Every cut I make along a main or subordinate branch is as close to the branch as possible so the cut can heal properly.

Figure W-14. I prune off most downward hanging branches, because they get little sunlight.

Figure W-15. Collecting and dragging prunings on a tarp is efficient, especially on slick snow.

PRUNING A STANDARD APPLE TREE

The key purpose of pruning a standard apple tree is to get as much direct sunlight to as many fruiting branches on the exterior of the tree as possible. The natural outcome of such pruning creates an open muscular set of branches that hold aloft more delicate smaller branches as well as their twigs and fruiting spurs. By the way—if you want fruit on your apple trees, be sure to plant at least two of each type to ensure cross-pollination.

Modern orchardists want nothing to do with these old broad, tall trees, which are utterly inefficient because their height and width make the harvest difficult. My brother Peter, who today runs the orchard where we grew up in northwestern Connecticut, has taken out all the old standard apple trees that we grew up pruning with our father and replaced them with semi-dwarf trees, which he prunes into tall, open pyramids. What I'm after, ornamental gardener that I am, is an old standard apple tree that has the outline of a big, open umbrella that looks beautiful and produces apples.

If you want to harvest fruit on these old, tall trees, you have to decide what your comfort level is with climbing ladders. Prune your tree to a height that's comfortable for you to climb. As you can see in Figure W-12, I use a 12-foot apple picking ladder to do most of my pruning up high, though I do admit to getting off the ladder and climbing around in the upper reaches of the 20-foot-high tree.

The basic approach, which can take anywhere from two to four hours to accomplish depending on the standard tree's size and condition, is to start with the obvious choices and work toward the more complex.

1. Remove the dead wood from the entire tree. You'll find most of it in the interior; apple branches don't grow well in shade. A dead branch's bark curls away from the woody stem; the ends have broken off.

2. When pruning live wood, start from the interior and work out. Inexperienced pruners start from the outside and work in.) Cut out vertical water sprouts that run along the inside trunks of the tree (see Figure W-13).

3. Remove inner branches that are totally shaded. In Figure W-14 I'm pruning a branch that is growing down rather than out and, as such, is shaded by branches above it.

4. Finally, thin out the remaining branches around the perimeter of the tree, keeping in mind that you want maximum sunlight to reach branches that will produce fruit. Imagine branches as arms holding apples to the sunlight. Also prune out thin, weak branches that cross above or below stronger, stouter ones.

To help you better understand step 4, look closely again at Figure W-12, the photo of the big apple tree in our garden. I have completed pruning the left two-thirds of the treetop but have not yet thinned the right third. As I pruned this tree, I kept in mind the weight of fruit that the branches will have to support. I cut back long, leggy branches to a junction point where the main branch and a stout secondary one diverge. I was also careful not to thin the outermost upper branches too aggressively; I don't want to allow too much winter sun to shine onto the top surfaces of the upper branches to create sunscald—a splitting of the bark.

Don't be afraid to make a few big cuts, particularly when you have large vertical water sprouts that have grown many branches over time. A regularly pruned apple tree responds remarkably well to some heavy pruning.

Pick up prunings periodically so you aren't tripping over them, especially when moving a heavy ladder with a saw in your hand and shears in your pocket. After you collect prunings, lay all of them in the same direction on a tarp so they stack tightly when you remove them for later burning. Then gather two corners of the tarp and pull it to the burn pile (see Figure W-15). Don't move on to the next tree until you have picked up prunings under the tree you just finished. That way you won't feel discouraged at the end of your work by how much cleanup there is.

At some point during July or August, I return to this apple tree with a ladder to summer-prune the water sprouts that invariably pop up along the stout inner branches (see Figure W-16). That's good husbandry, but it also helps the clean lines of the major trunks to stay simple.

PRUNING A CRAB APPLE TREE

A crab apple responds differently to pruning than does a standard apple tree. When you cut a branch of most crab apple trees, a number of latent buds break. If you make too many cuts at the ends of branches, the tree will look like a porcupine, which is how most crab apples across America look.

When it comes to thinning out exterior branches, I am as restrained when pruning a crab apple tree as I am aggressive with a standard apple, although I follow a similar sequence. After all, the purpose of pruning a crab apple is to get as many flowers and persistent fruit as possible (see Figure I-3 on page 13). Here's the sequence I follow.

1. I start by pruning out all the vertical water sprouts growing up from interior branches (see Figure W-17).
2. Next I prune out any interior branches that are growing back into the center of the tree (see Figure W-18).
3. I then go to the exterior and prune just a few branches that are shaded by overhanging branches (see Figure W-19). I also prune low branches that impede lawn mowing or walking. I don't want to thin out the exterior too much and give up all those flower buds and red or yellow fruits we enjoy seeing all winter.
4. I do not make any cuts at the ends of branches, to avoid an ungainly shape.
5. During the summer, I return to the crab

Figure W-16. Once or twice a summer I nip off water sprouts that grow along main branches.

once or twice to cut out vertical water sprouts as well as shoots coming up from the base of the tree (see Figure W-22 on page 34).

What results from this minimal pruning is the tree shown in Figure W-20: a crab apple with an open interior but quite thick branching and stems on the exterior. Compare the density of branches in the standard apple tree (Figure W-12)

Figure W-17. Many vertical water sprouts often shoot up or out wherever you make a cut on a crab apple tree, so prune with restraint.

Figure W-18. When pruning a crab apple, make most of the cuts on the interior. Here I am cutting a branch that is growing back into the tree's center.

Figure W-19. I do make a few cuts on the exterior, especially when a branch is totally shaded by overhanging larger branches.

Figure W-20. This is the look of a *Malus* 'Prairiefire' after I've finished pruning it: open interior, fairly dense exterior; no cuts at the tips of branches. Notice that the persistent fruit holding on since last summer is still on the tree in late March. Persistent fruit, along with disease resistance, are good qualities to look for when choosing a crab apple for your garden.

BRINGING UP POTS FROM THE COLD CELLAR

For years we tried growing tulips directly in garden beds, but moles, voles, and mice destroyed them. We decided to plant all our tulips in pots in autumn and overwinter them in the cold part of our cellar. If you don't have an unheated section of your cellar, store the pots in the garage. (More about this practice in the section on Autumn.) Early each April, I bring these pots out of the cellar just as the tulips are sending up their shoots. Our cat Onza knows that this signals the approach of spring mouse hunting.

Figure W-21. We have found that planting tulips in pots in soilless mix, and overwintering them in the cold cellar is the best way to avoid animal predation. When we plant tulip bulbs in the ground, mice and voles devour most of them.

Figure W-22. The base of our *Malus* 'Donald Wyman' sends up shoots from the rootstock. I cut off these shoots every month or so throughout the year. The only way to prevent such shoots from emerging is to plant a crab apple so the top of the root ball is an inch or two above grade. Even then, certain types of crab apples continue to send up these unsightly shoots

and that of the pruned crab apple (Figure W-17) and you'll see what I mean.

Many gardeners buy any crab apple and tell themselves they'll be able to prune it back to keep it small. If you want a small crab apple for a small garden, don't rely on pruning; rely on the garden-center owner to steer you to a crab apple that has been bred to mature at a certain height and width. For example, if you have a small garden and want a small crab apple tree for it, purchase *Malus* 'Tina,' a tree bred to mature at 6 feet high and wide, or the new *Malus* 'Lollipop', which matures at 10 feet high and wide.

Pruning Vines and Shrubs

PRUNING GRAPEVINES

The basic rule here is to prune back a tangle (see Figure W-23) hard to the shape of a five-fingered hand (or something like that, as shown in Figure W-24). Do this in the dead of winter before any sap starts running. If you prune a grapevine even in mid-March here in Vermont, the wounds will bleed sap for days. Here's the sequence I follow to disentangle a grapevine and get it ready for spring.

1. Get in among the branches and study the tangle for several minutes to make distinctions between primary, secondary, and tertiary branches, live wood from dead wood, old wood from new wood. If you study what appears to be a tangle in Figure W-23, you'll see how a grapevine in all its parts grows.
2. Start by removing dead wood. You can identify old dead wood by its decidedly flaking bark, as well as the white fungi that might be growing on it. You can also tell young dead wood by its barkless beige look. You'll see both in Figure W-23 if you look closely.

Figure W-23. In late February, before the sap begins to flow, prune grapevines. First study the tangle to select branchless, flaky deadwood from live wood, then find about five primary shoots. **Figure W-24.** Cut these shoots back hard, then remove all of the preceding year's growth. You want to end up with about five 2- to 3-foot-long stemless branches.

3. Next find the main trunk and follow the five to seven major vines that grow out from it. Cut each of those back to about 5 feet from the main trunk.

4. Remove all the resulting brush so you can see what remains to be done. In Figure W-24, I'm snipping small twigs from one of the five main vines.

5. What you end up with is a main trunk with a few 5-foot-long branchless vines.

Pruning a grapevine is pretty dramatic, because you remove so much of the plant, but that's what it takes. Be brave.

TYING UP RATHER THAN PRUNING

The flopping branches of many fastigiate (tall, narrow) trees should be tied up rather than pruned off. We have a fastigiate Colorado blue spruce (*Picea pungens* 'Glauca Fastigiata') in the garden that looks best when all its branches ascend to form a tight columnar outline. Each late winter I have to return to that tree to tie unobtrusive coated green wire or string around its perimeter to hold the branches in place. Tying up the flopping branches of some evergreens is often a better solution than pruning.

PRUNING A TRUMPET VINE

Pruning a trumpet vine (*Campsis radicans*) is a simple task, though a lot of gardeners don't do it and end up with an unsightly tangle year after year. Years ago I let the vine grow to about 15 feet in length, then cut off the tip. The vine has remained that length ever since. Every following January or February, I cut off last year's beige shoots right down to the nub (see Figure W-25). That's it.

Figure W-25. Every late February I cut back to the main vine all of the preceding year's shoots on a trumpet vine. New shoots emerge in spring.

BUILDING A BRUSH PILE

If you live in a densely populated suburban or urban area, avoid burning any brush. Call a landscaper or an arborist who has a chipper and have him or her dispose of your brush, or haul it yourself to a landfill or a recycling center where workers will chip the wood for you.

If you live in a rural or sparsely populated area, call your fire warden or fire department to secure permission to burn a brush pile. Then follow these directions to make a dense brush pile that you can burn or allow to decompose.

1. Select a place to pile brush that has 20 to 30 feet or so of open space around it, so when the fire starts it doesn't damage limbs or overhead wires.
2. Select a place that is not directly downwind from your house, so you avoid having smoke blow inside. By downwind, I mean the direction from which predominant winds blow.
3. Keep the pile small and manageable. It is much safer to burn several small piles 3 feet high and 6 feet across rather than a single but much larger pile.
4. Collect dry wood and stack the pieces parallel so they lie tightly with few air pockets. This deadwood will help you get the fire started later.
5. Lay all subsequent brush on top of the dried wood and parallel with it.

6. Cut up large branches so they lie tightly and fill in air pockets within the pile. Air pockets make a pile difficult to burn; without sufficient heat, the fire will not reach across a 2- to 3-foot air pocket.

7. You can throw wood onto your burn pile over the course of a few weeks. Mix green wood with dried wood; too much dry wood will generate a very hot fire, and too much sappy green wood will be difficult to burn.

Here are suggestions for burning the pile.

1. Call your fire warden for permission to burn the brush on a particular day.

2. Burn early in the day before the wind gets up; choose a day when a light rain is falling or there is snow on the ground.

3. Have a hose ready if the fire needs to be calmed down or put out.

4. Wear eye protection, a hat, gloves, long-sleeved shirt, and long pants.

5. Stay with the fire until it is extinguished.

6. Know that you can't simply light a fire and walk away. A fire needs to be tended, because only the wood near the center of the fire will burn; the edges of the pile will have to be pitchforked into the central area of heat.

7. Determine from which direction the wind is blowing by feeling the wind on your face or by lighting a small piece of newspaper and seeing which way the smoke blows.

8. Stuff newspaper and cardboard into a gap in the bottom of the pile, then force dried wood atop the kindling paper. Place the paper so that when it is lit, the wind will blow the fire directly into the brush pile.

9. Do not use accelerants such as gasoline or a rubber tire. Both are dangerous.

10. Once you have lit the paper, pile dried wood atop the fire to give it a good start.

11. Once the fire is going, you can direct its burn to some degree by piling dried wood and brush just ahead of the flames.

12. As the pile burns, push the sides in with a pitchfork, and add wood atop the center of the fire to keep it hot.

13. Once all the brush is burned, let the fire smolder as long as there is no wind that might blow coals or embers onto nearby grass.

14. Once the wood is burned, extinguish the remaining coals with the hose. Stir the ashes with a pitchfork to be sure you have extinguished all the coals.

15. A week or two after you have burned the brush pile, spread the ashes under a lilac, because it appreciates the alkaline nature of the ashes. Or spread the ashes atop your compost pile.

PRUNING MULTISTEMMED SHRUBS

Many shrubs send up multiple stems directly out of the ground (see Figure W-26) as opposed to those that send up a single stem that then send out branches. As a result, much of the pruning on multistemmed shrubs involves thinning out the interior as the plants' circumference expands

Figure W-26. Red-twig dogwood—ours is *Cornus alba* 'Elegantissima'—as with yellow-twig dogwood, sends up shoots from a central crown. Every spring I use well-sharpened lopping shears to remove older graying stems. Latent buds near the cuts then break in spring and give rise to new brightly colored shoots, which look attractive in our winter garden, especially with an evergreen backdrop.

over the years. The way I prune a red-twig dogwood (see Figure W-26) holds pretty well for shrubs with a similar growth habit. That is, with lopping shears or a pruning saw, I reach into the interior to first remove all the dead wood, then I thin out the older main stems by cutting just a few of them each year to keep young growth coming. You can do this with lilac, mockorange (*Philadelphus coronarius*), and many other shrubs that have this growth habit.

PRUNING SINGLE-STEMMED SHRUBS WITH MANY BRANCHES

Many shrubs, including rhododendron, lily-of-the-valley shrub (*Pieris japonica*), a mountain laurel (*Kalmia latifolia*), send up one to three stems, which then branch out well above the ground. To prune these, work from the inside out. At almost anytime of the year except spring get down on your hands and knees, part the branches, and look carefully inside the shrub to decide which branches are dead. Cut them out. Then cut branches that cross others or are so deep within the plant that they get no sun (see Figure W-27). Also cut some of the lower branches that touch the ground. The goal is to get sunlight to most of the branches and to open the interior so you can see the attractive branching habit.

PRUNING A BURNING BUSH: A STORY

Dymock Maurice, a client of mine years ago, was a tall, trim Englishwoman of handsome bearing and nearly eighty years old. She had a summer home just across the river from us in Walpole, New Hampshire. I was working in her garden one early summer day when she came out to ask for my help with the always rampant burning bush (*Euonymus alatus* 'Compactus') in the middle of her lawn. It was about 20 feet high and wide, and she wanted me to prune it back.

I told her that fall would be a better time, once its leaves had fallen, but she would have none of that. I held my breath and pruned back the shrub by almost half; the result was a motley collection of 10-foot-long leafless branches. Dymock came out to look over the results of my work and asked, "Did you bring your chain saw?" I fetched it, and she showed me where she had tied a ribbon about 3 feet above the ground around one branch. "That's the height I want the whole shrub to be cut back to." I was not going to argue with an Englishwoman who had likely been gardening for at least sixty years.

By the time I finished, I had reduced a 20-foot shrub to a 3-footer; it was not a pretty sight. A year later I went back to help with some other work, and there was the burning bush—a dense 4-foot-high mounding shrub covered with leaves and flourishing to a fare-thee-well, thank you very much.

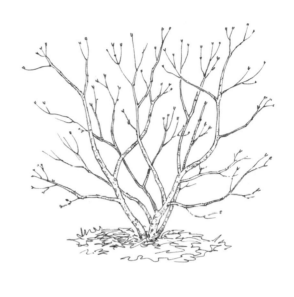

Pruning Shrub   E. Scaw

Figure W-27. Remove branches that cross others and shade too much of the shrub's interior.

How to Create a New Coppice

1. Choose a section of meadow, an area of your existing garden dominated by overgrown shrubs, or an area at the edge of a woodland.
2. Remove all aggressive perennial weeds and grasses, then cultivate the area, perhaps with a rototiller.
3. Either coppice existing overgrown shrubs, or plant native woody species that are appropriate for coppicing (see the list on page 46), such as sumac, red-twig dogwood, maple and oak, roughly 6 feet on center in big sweeps, or as single accent specimens.
4. Incorporate climbers such as species and wild roses, honeysuckle, and clematis among coppiced shrubs.
5. Mass-plant perennials such as rudbeckia, goldenrod, and others associated with meadows, or, in shady areas, plant spring-blooming perennials and bulbs.
6. Weed the first year and perhaps the second to give the perennials a chance to get established.
7. Wait three years or so until sufficient root systems have developed in the woody shrubs, then coppice them.
8. Once the entire planting is established, it can be cut to ground level late every winter, and it will rebound every spring.

Coppicing

If you have ever used a chain saw to cut broad-leaved trees or shrubs to within 2 to 3 inches of the ground to clear a view or a woodland path, you probably watched with dismay over the next few months as a thicket of shoots grew from the stumps you left. In fact, what you did was to coppice the woody plants. For centuries in Europe, coppicing has been used to rejuvenate overgrown plants. It's a method you can use to manage a maturing garden.

You can coppice rangy shrubs in overgrown gardens to bring light and air into a former tangled shady mass of twigs and branches, under which nothing will grow. The result of such severe pruning is that the ground underneath, newly opened to sunlight, can support not only flowering perennials and bulbs but new shoots with bright new stems of the shrub itself, such as those of red- or yellow-twig dogwood, many viburnums such as wayfaring tree (*Viburnum lantana* 'Mohican'), sumac, burning bush, and forsythia.

Although many plants succumb to the radical pruning required for coppicing—you basically cut it to the ground—there are many that respond well. See the lists of suitable plants on page 46, or do some local research before carrying out such drastic pruning.

If you do decide to coppice a shrub, be brave. Half measures will be worse than the full treatment. Cut the shrub to within 2 inches of the ground and you'll get a good balance of shoots on the perimeter of the stump. If you lose your nerve and cut the many stems of a shrub a foot

Figure W-28. Pollarding a willow of virtually any age can dramatically reduce its size. Try this on any overgrown willows in your garden.

or more off the ground, you'll get a tangle of interior shoots, and latent buds on the exterior will not "break." You will have the most success coppicing shrubs and trees that have been growing in place for at least three to five years. Younger or very old shrubs, such as old woody roses, will respond to coppicing with far fewer shoots, or they may even give up the ghost. Allow new shoots from a coppiced shrub to grow as they will for the first year; during the second and subsequent years, thin out the weaker shoots and leave the stronger ones.

POLLARDING

Pollarding is coppicing a tree 8 feet or so up its trunk. It's an old European technique that we use to keep willows under control and still enjoy

their silvery look hovering above the garden (see Figure W-28). You could do the same with your weeping willows, linden, some oaks, ash, catalpa, or other trees listed on page 46 that accept pollarding. It's a simple process for young, recently planted trees.

About ten years ago we planted five white willows (*Salix alba*) with main stems that were only as thick as a pencil and a couple of feet high. After five years, the trees were 12 feet tall and had about a 1½-inch-thick trunk. Once the trees got to that size, I went into the garden in early March with a ladder, a pair of pruning shears, and a saw. I simply cut off the trunk of each tree 8 feet above the ground and snipped off all the branches below that height.

In early spring of that year, latent buds within the thin bark of the tree emerged, and many young branches formed, especially at the top of the trunk. I nipped or rubbed off the few buds that broke between ground level and about 7 feet up the trunk, while allowing breaking buds at the very top of the trunk to grow. After several weeks, thirty to forty branches had grown about 3 feet long. As a group they formed a kind of open sphere of wispy branches and silvery foliage atop the otherwise leafless 7-foot-high trunk (see Figure W-28).

Every March since then, I have gone out to the five silver willow pollards (see Figure W-29) and gotten on a ladder to prune last year's stems (see Figure W-30). As you can see, I leave 2- to 3-inch stubs, along which buds emerge in early spring.

You could also plant young trees (from the list on page 46) that will accept pollarding, and pollard them later. Three years ago, for example, I designed a garden for clients in New Hampshire. We planted several 2-inch-diameter sycamores (*Platanus × acerifolia* 'Bloodgood') and allowed the trees to grow unpruned for three years. In March of the fourth year, when the base of most of the main branches where they meet the trunk was at least 1½ inches in diameter, we

Figure W-29. (Opposite) This is a willow one year after I pollarded it. **Figure W-30.** This is the same willow as in Figure W-29 after pruning it. I could instead have pruned the nubs back to the main trunk, and new shoots would have emerged.

SOME SHRUBS AND TREES FOR COPPICING

Alder
Ash
Black locust
Chestnut
Elm, especially *Ulmus glabra*
Escallonia rubra
Eucalyptus
Forsythia
Fragrant viburnum (*Viburnum farreri*)
Hazel
Holly
Linden
Maple
Oak, particularly Holm oak
Ornamental bramble
Poplar
Red- and yellow-twig dogwood
  (*Cornus alba* 'Sibirica')
Sumac
Wayfaring tree (*Viburnum lantana*)

SOME TREES FOR POLLARDING

Ash	**Hornbeam**
Beech	**Linden**
Black locust	**London plane**
Catalpa	**Oak**
Elm	**Empress tree** (*paulownia*)
Fruitless mulberry	**Sweet chestnut**
Gingko	**Willow**

sawed the branches back to 1-foot stubs. Latent buds broke in spring, and now globe-shaped masses of branch and foliage appear each summer.

As you can imagine, coppicing and pollarding require a stout heart, a sharp saw, and a leap of faith. But if you can muster all three, you can rejuvenate appropriate shrubs, bring an overgrown shrub back into scale, create a whole new look for some of your trees, and bring sunlight, warmth, and color to previously shaded ground.

TRAINING TREES AND SHRUBS TO ASSUME CERTAIN SHAPES

Many trees that accept pollarding will also accept training (see Figure W-31). Here you see our beech tunnel made from saplings of *Fagus sylvatica* that we planted many years ago when their trunks were about an inch in diameter. We planted a sapling at the base of either side of each rebar arch, and over the years have tied the sapling to the arching rebar. Every winter since planting them, and two or three times during the summer, I've pruned these saplings on the inside and outside to form the tunnel you see here. The beech tree is such a powerful grower, you can't go wrong.

Figure W-31. After five years of training, these purple-leaved beech saplings have formed a tunnel—a pleasing transition from one garden area to the next.

THE TARPAULIN

Simple tools are best, and what could be simpler than a tarpaulin? Over the last fifteen years of working in our own garden in southern Vermont, I have learned how useful a simple garden tarp can be, and how simplicity lends itself to versatility.

One morning years ago, I pulled into our driveway with a load of shrubs on my pickup truck. As I untied the 8- by 10-foot woven polyethylene tarp that I had used to protect the shrubs during transport, I was thinking ahead to the planting that I would do that day and the mess I would make on the lawn paths between the borders where the shrubs were going.

I had plastic sheeting in the garden shed, but I knew from experience that before long I'd tear it with my shovel and end up with soil and roots and peat moss scattered everywhere. Then I realized that I could use the tarpaulin instead. It was of generous dimensions, it was strong and slippery enough to be dragged along the ground when laden with soil and debris, and it was tough—I wouldn't easily tear it with the point of my shovel.

I spread the tarp to overlap the edge of the garden by a foot or so, then started planting. An hour later the tarp was strewn with burlap wrapping, twine, soil, stones, weeds, compost, prunings, and plant labels. I shoveled what soil and compost I could back into the border, then pulled the tarp to the compost and nearby burn pile and sorted out the wood, the plastic, and the compostable materials. What I left behind in the garden was an area of lawn that was just as clean as when I had begun work.

Several days later I was weeding a broad perennial bed in the garden. Rather than use the wheelbarrow, a raised 2- by 3-foot target enclosed on three sides, I spread out an 8- by 10-foot tarp. It didn't take me long to realize what good aim a wheelbarrow requires, and how missing the target would break my concentration on the job at hand. A large tarp lying on the ground is hard to miss and holds a lot of weeds; and it's at ground level, so I don't need to twist or raise my body to aim weeds into a wheelbarrow or a bucket.

After completing the weeding in one section of the border, I simply pulled the tarp to the next section and loaded more weeds on it. When the tarp held what I felt I could comfortably pull, I lifted each of the four corners in turn to gather the weeds at the center. Then I twisted two of the corners together to give me a firm grip on the tarp, and hauled the whole thing to the compost pile (see Figure W-15 on page 29, in which I am hauling away prunings on a tarp; it's the same idea).

To unload the tarp, I just pull at one end of it and roll the weeds and debris onto or next to the compost pile. The only problem I've found is that in my enthusiasm to get the work done, I sometimes overload the tarp. When a wheelbarrow is too full, you can see that, but a tarp is too full only when you can't pull it without straining yourself. If you're not paying attention, you'll load it well beyond that point.

Of course, there are any number of other uses to which a garden tarp can be put.

- To ease cleanup when a load of sand, gravel, mulch, or compost must be delivered onto a lawn or driveway.
- To cover materials such as plants, sand, leaves, or loose compost when hauling them in a pickup truck.
- To collect and haul away leaves.
- To carry mulch or compost into tightly planted shrub or flower borders. With the aid of another person, you can sift the mulch off the edge of the tarp and in between the tightly spaced plants.
- To catch twigs and prunings when trimming a hedge, shrub, or tree.
- To collect debris when dividing or transplanting perennials.
- To collect leaves or branches as they are spit from a shredder or chipper.
- To cover tools and equipment that need to be left out.

You can buy inexpensive polyethylene garden tarps, either laminated or open weave, with or without grommets (reinforced holes through which pass tie-down cords), in several colors, sizes, and weights, from mail-order catalogs, garden centers, and discount centers. Tarps come 6 by 8 feet to 12 by 16 feet and cost between three and ten dollars, depending on their size; I have several different ones for different jobs. More recently, I've purchased industrial-strength PVC tarps; they're longer lasting than poly tarps but definitely weigh more and cost at least sixfold more per square yard.

I have found the 8- by 10-foot size to be most versatile, but you'll want to match the tarp to the job. You could fill a 10- by 16-foot tarp with leaves and haul it easily, but cover such a large tarp with heavy debris from transplanting, and you won't be able to budge it.

I prefer unlaminated tarps when working on a slope because they are not nearly as slippery, so weeds and debris stay where they land. Yet slippery, laminated tarps are easier to pull along a level lawn and to unload.

There are tarps made of other materials, but these create more problems than they solve. Burlap is difficult to pull along the ground, and it seems to catch on every root or stone in sight; furthermore, burlap is heavy when wet, can mildew, and wears out quickly. Canvas that has been treated with a waterproofing substance is much heavier than polyethylene and, like burlap, can mildew. Clear plastic tears too easily, and it is so light that it riffles in even a modest breeze, disrupting the flow of your work.

There are clearly many more uses for tarps that you will discover as you work around your place. When you begin working with a garden tarp or any other tool, you may well come to the same conclusion I've reached: once you bring an open and creative mind to the job at hand, you realize that simple tools are versatile tools.

■ CHECKLISTS

LATE AUTUMN/EARLY WINTER

- Burn the brush pile.
- Mulch trees, shrubs, and perennials that you planted during the preceding season.
- If you planted a boxwood, yew, or other evergreen hedge, or broad-leaved evergreens, during the preceding season, spray them with an antidessicant in early November, and set up burlap on their south side to prevent too much sunlight from drying out foliage.
- Keep snow from building up on branches of evergreens throughout the winter.
- Have power equipment serviced.
- If you live in Zone 4 or colder, cut pine or spruce boughs and cover your perennial beds with them in late November. This practice will keep the soil reliably frozen throughout the winter, so the crowns of plants will not be heaved out of the ground by freeze-thaw cycles.

■ CHECKLISTS

LATE WINTER

- Sharpen any tools with blades—such as pruners, lopping shears, and hedge shears—as well as shovels and hoes.
- Get new handles put on broken tools.
- Assess your tools and place orders for new ones or replacements.
- Keep snow from piling up on evergreens.
- Pollard the willows.
- Prune crab apples.
- Prune standard apple trees, pear trees, and other fruit trees.
- Assess the branches of trees and shrubs hanging over beds or paths; decide which branches need to be removed for easier access or for more light. Remove them.
- Prune maples, yellowwoods, and grapevines in January, or early February at the latest; these and certain other woody plants will bleed if pruned when the spring surge of sap is running.
- Cut back old graying stems of red-twig dogwood.
- Cut back ornamental grasses.
- Cut down trees that need removing.
- Prune trumpet vines.
- Retie trees or shrubs you are training to retain their look.
- Check all evergreens for winter damage; tie up any flopping branches on fastigiate blue spruce, arborvitae, and other upright evergreens.
- Once a month, water tulips planted in pots and stored in the cold cellar or garage.
- Start any garden design work early, so you can place orders for plants or materials in a timely fashion.

Managing Ornamental Grasses

Here are a few pointers regarding how to manage and cut back large-scale ornamental grasses such as this overwintered purple-reed grass (*Miscanthus sinensis* 'Purpurascens').

- We leave some of the stouter grasses, such as maiden grass and fountain grass standing for the winter, especially if they are in sight of key windows in the house. Otherwise, we cut them back just to save time in spring. To cut them back, sweep your hand and arm around a whole clump, then with pruning shears cut an armful of stems at a time, leaving about a 12-inch stubble, which will help support the coming season's grass stems. Another method is to tie a loop of rope around a clump of grass 12 inches or so above ground to provide tension, then cut just below the rope with a chain saw.

- A friend encouraged us to simply set fire to our clumps of ornamental grasses in autumn. One fall we did that with several *Miscanthus* grasses. How dramatic! How easy! But the following summer, the new growth on the grasses that we burned was far more vulnerable to heavy rains, which caused the stems to flop badly, whereas the grasses with the supporting 12-inch stems that resulted from cutting back stood straighter. Our lesson: don't burn grasses.

Figure W-32. When cutting back grasses, I leave 12-inch stubble. Dry and stout, it supports the following year's growth.

Spring

Figure SP-1. (Opposite) Early April in front of our garden shed looking into the herb garden. **Figure SP-3.** Daffodils and Virginia bluebells (*Mertensia virginica*) in the Woodland Garden.

THE WEEKS BETWEEN THE END OF WINTER and the beginning of spring in the Northeast form *the* cusp of the gardener's year. We look back with longing at the respite offered by four to five months of winter, a sedentary time when we catch our breath, go to garden symposia, read, and not have to pull a single, solitary weed. At the same time we look forward to seeing the last of the snow, the first of the bulbs. More than once in late March or early April, I've groused about the lingering patches of snow and gone out with shovel in hand to scatter the cold white stuff onto lawn and driveway (see Figure SP-1) to hasten its disappearance, knowing that in a few weeks all the snow will have melted anyway (see Figure 1 on page 6).

Once the snow is gone, there is a remarkably short time before the emergence of bulbs and perennials, yet there's *so much to do*—so much that I find myself raking right up to the edge of retreating snow. I can't wait. No matter what the common wisdom is regarding when to open up beds in spring, I'm right there where snow meets open soil, albeit mindful not to walk on the sodden, easily compacted ground.

Figure SP-4. Blue and white woodland phlox (*Phlox divaricata*) blanket the Woodland Garden in mid- to late April. **Figure SP-5.** (Opposite) The Entry Garden in mid-May: tulips in pots, crab apples in bloom, spring in full swing.

I'm raking sodden leaves that blew in during the winter especially where daffodils and Virginia bluebells (*Mertensia virginica*) will be poking through any minute (see Figure SP-1). The leaves are wet and heavy from the melting snow, so the raking isn't easy. We're pulling the first weeds of our seven-month growing season, picking up broken branches and sticks from beds and lawn, cleaning the garden shed, putting out the garden furniture and ornaments, and, with a ball

cart, hauling up from the cold cellar the large terra-cotta pots that Mary and I planted with tulips last October.

And then there's the edging, something I haven't had time to attend to since last August. In mid- to late April, once the lawn is no longer sodden, and before the perennials along bed edges have grown much, we can see the line where lawn meets bed. We like crisp, dropped edges. They clearly define the shape of bed and lawn; they establish a frame and keep lawn grasses from creeping into beds. With edges cut, we can feel and see the launching of the new gardening season.

And then, before we know it, the spring gardens, raked and edged, are awash in color. In the Woodland Garden (see Figure SP-4) are woodland phlox (*Phlox divaricata*), *Phlox stolonifera*, foamflower (*Tiarella cordifolia*), bloodroot, daffodils, crocus, columbine, brunnera, bleeding heart, pulmonaria, viola, primula, wild oats (*Uvularia grandiflora*), bergenia, and aurinias. Tulips are in their pots by the entrance to the garden (see Figure SP-5). And above them, in bloom, are magnolias, Cornell Pink azalea (*Rhododendron mucronulatum*) (see Figure SP-6), forsythia, cherries, shadblow, pieris, azalea, and even *Acer pseudosieboldiana*, periwinkle (*Vinca minor* 'Bowles') blooms below.

TOOLS WE CAN'T DO WITHOUT

We rely on certain garden tools that work for us:

- **Dutch wheelbarrow, with its light plastic barrow**
- **Felco #2 pruning shears for Gordon; Felco #6s for Mary's smaller hands**
- **5-gallon bucket, to carry into the beds when weeding or collecting small sticks and other debris**
- **Large tarpaulin spread on the ground to hold weeds, sticks, and other debris that can then be dragged to the burn or compost piles**
- **Hand hoe**
- **Rubber-palmed gloves with cloth backs for Mary**
- **Goatskin gloves made by the Green Mountain Glove Company, in Randolph, Vermont, from supple yet tough goatskin imported from Afghanistan. I think they're the finest work gloves known to man.**
- **Waterproof Muck Boots, to keep our feet dry**
- **Hats, to protect our heads from overhead thorns, branches, and the sun**

Figure SP-6. (Opposite) In the Spring Garden, Cornell Pink azalea (*Rhododendron mucronulatum*) blooms above, primulas and daffodils below.

Figure SP-7. Dragging the rake tines along the ground isn't as effective as flipping the tines, as Siena is doing here. Active flipping scoops up all the leaves, not just some of them.

Cleanup

We get one quick start in spring. We don't want matted leaves inhibiting the growth of daffodils, especially because their stems and buds often grow right up through the snow. And as the snow recedes, we pick up sticks, pluck leaves out of evergreen and deciduous woody plants, and generally take stock of a messy garden. We also cut back grasses and other perennials we left up for winter interest and prune deadwood from woody plants, such as Russian sage (*Perovskia atriplicifolia*). We rake all the lawns once the soil has dried out a bit, sweep stone paths and terraces, and place garden furniture and ornaments that have been stored in the barn all winter.

MANAGING LEAVES: RAKING

Stop to ask yourself why you are raking leaves in spring. You may have to rake, or you may not. There's no need, for example, to rake leaves from under many shrubs with overarching branches, such as stephanandra or other shrubs in a woodland garden. Those leaves, hidden from sight by branching, will decompose on their own, provide nutrients for the plants, and keep weeds down. On the other hand, if you've underplanted lilacs in the garden proper with bulbs

Figure SP-8. The garden is messy when all the snow has melted.

Figure SP-9. We rake leaves onto the lawn, then I collect them with the leaf mulcher attachment on my lawn tractor. **Figure SP-10.** Robin rakes leaves directly onto a tarp, because I can't collect leaves on such a pea-stone surface with the mulcher attachment on my lawn tractor.

and ferns, remove leaves under those shrubs to allow herbaceous plants to come up unfettered.

To make leaf raking manageable in spring, we work hard in autumn to get up as many leaves as possible. Even with all that work, though, the garden needs a lot of attention in spring (see Figure SP-8). Leaves that are dry and lightweight in fall are wet and heavy in spring. What we want to avoid is what we had to deal with one year when Mother Nature threw us a mighty curveball. Even before all the leaves had fallen from the trees in late October, a foot of snow fell, then again in early November, thereby preventing us from completing the leaf raking. The following spring the leaves were too wet and matted to be raked; we had to peel back sheets of them from hundreds of square yards of beds to allow bulbs and perennials to grow and the earth to breathe. It was cold, hard work. The lesson? Get those leaves up in early autumn.

DAFFODILS SIGNAL THE START OF RAKING

Daffodils are a good indicator to time the first raking in spring. When daffodils start poking through, we start raking. That's usually the first week of April in southern Vermont. If you wait to rake until the daffodil shoots are 2 to 3 inches high, you'll snap off the tender tips.

We also aim to rake all the perennial beds before the early daylily and peony shoots appear. This way we can walk on the beds and not damage young shoots. If we wait to rake even a few days after the shoots begin to appear, the rake tines break the tender shoots, and our boots crush them.

We start raking as early in the morning as we can before the winds kick up. Leaf raking in the calm early morning hours means that the leaves don't blow around. Furthermore, we start at the side of the garden from which the wind will blow—in our case we start on the west beds and rake toward the east—so if winds kick up, they won't blow loose leaves back onto what we just raked.

WHICH RAKE TO USE, HOW TO USE IT

Siena, one of the women helping in our garden, tells us that she likes to use a flexible plastic rake on lawns but prefers a firmer rake with metal or stout wire tines for teasing leaves out of perennial beds, where the stems of hardy geraniums, for example, remain throughout the winter and hold leaves. A metal rake acts more like a comb than does a plastic rake. Pat Sanzone, another of our garden helpers, keeps rakes that have lost their middle tines. She finds them useful when raking on either side of a crown of a perennial, or at the base of a small shrub, without damaging the spring shoots.

The action that takes best advantage of a rake's springy tines is not to drag it but to make a series of small quick jabs in succession (see Figure SP-7). The springing action enables you to flip leaves ahead and directly onto a 10- by 10-foot tarp (see Figure SP-10). Once the tarp is full, we draw two corners together, twist the corners to form a handle, and drag the tarp to the compost pile, being careful to separate sticks and prunings from more easily compostable materials such as leaves or weeds.

Figure SP-11. During the initial spring raking, we don't aim to get every leaf, because more will blow in with the April winds. We just want to get the matted bulk of leaves off tender shoots.

There are a variety of rakes available:

- 24- to 32-inch-wide plastic rake with a wooden handle for lawn raking
- 18- to 24-inch-wide metal rake with a metal or wooden handle with stiff tines, useful for teasing leaves out of perennials
- 8- to 12-inch-wide hand rake for getting into tight places or under small shrubs
- adjustable-width aluminum rake for a variety of garden chores

USE THE WIND

I take advantage of light breezes or even a wind. I always start raking upwind and work downwind of my leaf pile; the movement of the wind supports the action of the rake and helps push leaves toward the tarp. The action of the wind can also be a real problem if it blows leaves all over the place. Given this, I rarely rake leaves into several piles, then go back to gather them. I rake one tarpful of leaves and haul it to the composting spot, then go back to rake more leaves and fill the tarp again. Rake and remove. If you rake and leave the piles overnight or even for an hour, you'll find a lot of leaves scattered back on the lawn, and you will have wasted your efforts.

I always store leaves downwind of the garden. When we make leaf piles to the west of the garden, strong northwest winds often blow a small but annoying percentage of the leaves right back onto it.

We rake leaves in two stages over the course of the spring.

Figure SP-12. Once Robin has completed raking the periwinkle, she goes back to handpick leaves from among this dense evergreen plant.

1. The first raking in early April gets the bulk of the leaves that blew onto the beds after we decided enough is enough last fall. We don't want wet, matted leaves to hamper the growth of bulbs or herbaceous perennials. We know that detail raking and leaf removal will not be worth it this early in spring, because winds will carry in more leaves, so we aren't too picky about getting up every single leaf (see Figure SP-11).

2. We then wait two to three weeks, until the shoots of grasses and wild daylilies to the west of our garden are up 6 to 8 inches, so they trap and hold leaves in place, thereby preventing them from being blown onto the garden. It's then that we can begin finicky leaf removal throughout the garden (see Figure SP-12).

CLEANING LAWN WITH LAWN TRACTOR AND MULCHER ATTACHMENT

I cannot abide the sound of a leaf blower. Although I recognize that it saves a lot of labor and enables you to get leaves out of tricky corners and from between the shoots of shrubs, and it's especially good in fall when leaves are dry, I simply won't buy one. Besides, they're useful in spring only once the leaves have dried out.

To help with leaf removal, I purchased a leaf mulcher for my riding lawn mower (see Figure SP-13) ten years ago. I find this to be of inestimable help. We rake the beds almost free of leaves and collect them on the lawn (see Figures SP-9 and SP-11). If they aren't too wet or piled

Figure SP-13. Whenever possible we rake leaves onto the lawn; then I can easily pick them up with the mulcher attachment on my lawn tractor. We then compost the collected leaves.

Figure SP-14. Once we've raked the leaves, the shapes of the beds are clearer, although they still need to be edged.

more than a few inches high, I chop them up with the mulcher (see Figure SP-13), then drive the results to the compost pile. Mulched leaves break down fast.

MAKING AND MAINTAINING EDGES IN THE GARDEN

Edges sharpen the image of your garden, and they also reduce maintenance. Without edging between beds and lawn, grass and clover creep in among perennials, and before you know it you have the daunting task of taking up an entire garden to extricate the grass. Furthermore, linear or broadly curving edges are far easier to mow than those that wiggle and squiggle in and out of the bed. You can edge a bed with brick, stone, steel, or even gravel and pea stone. By covering the often weedy meeting point between lawn and garden with stone or brick laid horizontally, you reduce the amount of weeding required to keep your beds looking good. Furthermore, your lawn mower, one wheel of which can ride on the broad horizontal edging, doesn't clip the outer foliage of the perennials at the edge of the bed, so your garden looks well tended. The one method of edging that I explain in detail (below) is the dropped edge, one that we use almost exclusively in our garden, in part because it is free but for the work it requires.

THE DROPPED LAWN EDGE

Each spring, after we have raked the lawn and beds free of leaves (see Figure SP-14), we edge

Figure SP-15. Patricia followed a string held taut at either end of this bed with bamboo stakes to get a straight edge. She used the D-handled straight-nosed spade to do this work.

each bed where it meets lawn. It takes four of us a day to a day and a half. This fact brings up an important point for you, dear reader. You may not want to spend even three hours edging let alone a day and a half with three helpers. This is my own craziness. Just take what you want from this section on edging and apply it to whatever amount of edging you're comfortable doing.

We start the day by gathering together many balls of twine, bamboo stakes, and a tape measure as well as three straight-nosed spades. These

Qualities to Look for in a Straight-Nosed Spade

A straight-nosed spade is pictured on page 65 (Figure SP-15).

- Shaft length appropriate for your height
- D- or T-shaped handle, which helps you push the blade into the sod
- Strong, solid meeting between wooden shaft and metal blade
- Truly straight-edged blade
- Forged, not stamped, blade with a slightly tapered bottom edge that can be readily sharpened
- Blade made from one piece of high-quality, unpainted steel (no welds), which will hold a sharp edge
- Good balance between light weight and sturdy construction

are spades with straight blades (see Pat's in Figure SP-15), not cupped like shovel blades, so we can produce a straight edge rather than the scalloped edge that a regular cupped shovel blade would produce.

Exactly where edges will go is the first step in getting the edges right. As you can see in Figure SP-16, we stake twine to bamboo stakes to establish where the edges will go, then I confirm the placement with a tape measure to determine the width of the first of three crab apple beds. I make sure the strings mark the same width for the next two beds. The string not only records the dimension of the beds but their alignment relative to one another. Look closely at Figure SP-17 and you'll see that the inner ends of the six beds in our crab apple orchard are not only straight in

and of themselves but parallel to one another. That's because we stretched the twine across several related beds rather than just along one separate bed and then the next. Once I confirm string placement, we begin cutting the edges by laying the back of the straight-nosed spade against the string and pushing the shovel down about 4 inches into the moist spring soil (see Figure SP-18).

We create a dropped lawn edge by removing just a sliver of sod, thereby creating an open space between bed edge and remaining lawn; grass roots will not travel into open air, so we have installed a de facto barrier against roots. We simultaneously create a crisp edge to the bed (see Figure SP-21) that sharpens the look of the whole place. If you're prepared to edge every

Figure SP-16. In the six-bed crab apple orchard, we lay out strings using a tape measure so all the lines of adjacent beds are parallel with one another.

Figure SP-17. We then cut the edges with the straight-nosed spade following the strings we held taut with bamboo stakes.

Figure SP-18. Because we have heavy clay soil that, along any bed edge, stays in place underfoot, we hold the angle of the spade virtually vertical. Where the is soil sandy, we would cut at a more oblique angle, as in Figure SP-19.

spring and maintain the edge with a string trimmer or edging shears, this is an inexpensive way to create a classy look that keeps beds free of grass and clover. And if you have guests coming for dinner over the weekend and the garden is looking a little worse for wear, take an afternoon to edge your beds; they'll look a million times better.

THE ANGLE OF THE CUT

Before cutting turf, take a close look at your soil to see how well it will stand up to a dropped edge. Family and guests will want to walk right up to the edge of your beds to smell the roses, so you want the soil at the edge to support their weight without collapsing. When working in

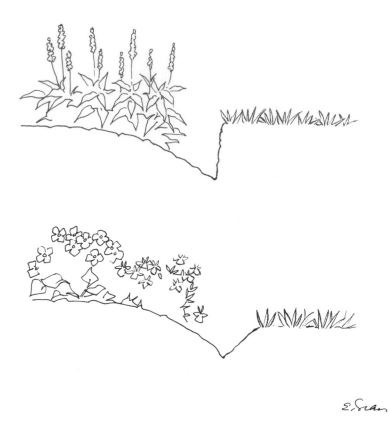

Figure SP-19. If you have heavy clay soil, as we do, you can cut a 3- to 4-inch nearly vertical dropped edge along a bed, because the heavy soil will support a person's weight. If you have sandy or moist soil, which would collapse underfoot, make only a 2- to 3-inch edge at a more oblique angle.

crumbly loam or sandy soil, both of which break down fairly easily underfoot, set your edging shovel at a 100-degree angle or thereabouts to give the edge more support. By dropping the handle on your spade to cut the soil at such an angle, you'll leave what amounts to a buttress of soil to support the edge. And dig down no more than 2 inches or so (see Figure SP-19). That too will help support a person's weight. Heavy clay soil such as we have allows Pat to hold her spade handle almost perpendicular to the level lawn, thereby creating a 90-degree cut that can be as deep as 4 inches (see Figures SP-19 and SP-15).

Also pay attention to the condition of the soil the day you're edging. If the soil along a straight edge is so wet that it will give way underfoot, or so dry that it will crumble, place an 8- to 10-foot-long 1 × 6 inch board along your intended line and stand on it as you work. Move the spade along the board edge so that it acts as a guide. If you're creating curving edges, stand on a small piece of plywood set back a few inches from the edge. Once established, lawn edges must be clipped every two to three weeks; long-handled vertical-action edging shears are the tool for the job, though I sometimes cheat and use a string trimmer.

Figure SP-20. This part of our garden looks crisp after raking and edging.

Planting Trees and Shrubs

PLANTING TREES

Tree planting practices have changed radically over the past decade or two. Now that the dust has settled in arguments among researchers of such matters, three central changes to tree planting techniques are now widely accepted.

1. The hole you dig should be no deeper than the root ball and two to three times its width.
2. Once the tree's rootball is in the hole, you should backfill the hole using the same soil you dug up to make the planting hole.
3. You should plant the tree so its topmost roots are an inch or so above the adjacent grade.

The old way of planting a tree required that you dig a hole broader and deeper than the root ball, then add lots of compost, fertilizer, and other amendments to the backfill soil. Research has shown that such soil amendments "spoil" the tree. Shortly after planting, roots begin to form at the periphery of the root ball and grow happily into the rich, amended soil over the first and second years, so the tree flourishes. However, when these young roots reach the unamended native soil, as they must, they turn around, and head right back for more of the good stuff. Over time, the tree begins to backslide.

The root system of a tree is by no means a mirror image of its trunk and branching; it's much broader and more far-reaching, and closer to the surface, than had been previously thought. According to Ed Gilman, a nationally recognized expert on trees at the University of Florida, Gainesville, some trees send their roots out three times the distance between the trunk and the outer tips of the branches. So a tree with a 15-foot radius could have roots 45 feet out from the trunk in all directions. The best planting technique, then, is to dig a hole that is an inch or two less than the depth of the root ball (so the root ball rests on undisturbed soil and does not settle) and two to three times as wide as the root ball. Research has shown that all that loose soil enables rootlets growing horizontally to more easily penetrate it and catch hold. See Ed Gilman's "Do and Don't" schematic regarding the most up-to-date tree planting method (Figure SP-30).

Here is the sequence I follow when planting a small tree, in this case a shadblow (*Amelanchier* × *grandiflora* 'Autumn Brilliance'):

Figure SP-21. (Opposite) I reach one finger inside the top of the burlap that is wrapped around the root ball, and poke my finger around the trunk to get a sense of where the topmost root of the tree is. What sometimes happens is that a mechanized tree spade, which nurseries use to dig up large plants, pushes excess soil atop a root ball as it draws the tree out of the ground. You want to

position the root ball so that the topmost root, which is not necessarily the top of the root ball, is 1 to 2 inches above grade.

Figure SP-22. I measure that dimension with my shovel handle.

Figure SP-23. I check that dimension against the depth of the hole I've dug. Because of the roots remaining from an elm tree I cut down just an hour before these photographs were taken, I dug a hole that was not as wide as it should have been. The ideal hole should be three times the width of the root ball. So don't do what these photos show; do what Torben Larsen did with his backhoe, as you'll see in Figure 21. Next, we roll the tree into the hole with the burlap and wire cage in place, so the root ball does not break apart for lack of the support. The ball appears much higher than the adjacent lawn, but keep in mind that the knotted burlap and excess soil from the tree spade obscure the topmost root, which is what determines the finish grade. Once the tree is in the hole, I position its most handsome and broadest side so it can be seen from the windows of the house or from some other key vantage point. Trees have a front, back, and sides because of the way they are grown in nurseries, so pay attention.

Figure SP-24. Once the tree is positioned to show its good side and is at the right depth, I cut off the topmost burlap with a utility knife, and with wire cutters I remove as much of the wire cage as possible.

Figure SP-25. Torben Larsen, who installs my designs and helps out in our garden from time to time, removes all the excess soil atop the root ball until he exposes the topmost root. Look closely and you'll see moisture at the base of the tree trunk, which reveals that almost 2 inches of excess soil had to be removed before Torben got to the surface roots.

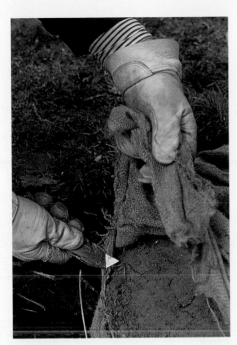

FIGURE SP-24

Figure SP-26. Next we backfill about two-thirds of the hole with the same soil we dug to make it.

Figure SP-27. We then water the soil well so that any air pockets we might not have seen are filled. If you backfill to the very top of the hole and then water, much of it will run off, so you can't be sure that water has reached the very bottom of the root ball. We complete the backfilling, being certain not to put any soil on top of the root ball, so the surface roots can do their job of providing oxygen to the plant.

FIGURE SP-25

FIGURE SP-26

FIGURE SP-27

FIGURE SP-28

FIGURE SP-29

Figure SP-28. Torben digs a hole with his backhoe that is three to four times the width of the root ball. That's the proper way to plant a tree. We always have a tarp or wheelbarrow nearby when planting. Rather than throw soil onto the lawn, we put it in the barrow or on the tarp to ease cleanup.

Figure SP-29. Torben shapes a 4-inch-high water well around the outer perimeter of the root ball then mulches the root ball and water well with 2 inches of leaf mold.

Figure SP-30. When planting a tree or shrub from a nursery, remove the wire and burlap as best you can, and plant the tree or shrub so the top of the root ball is 1 to 2 inches above the adjacent grade. Never put any soil on the top of the root ball as you backfill. (After Dr. Ed Gilman)

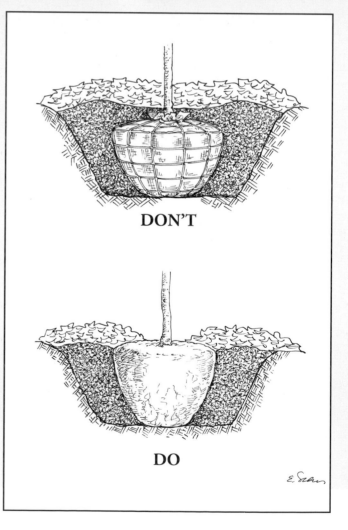

DON'T

DO

Figure SP-31. Torben covers the root ball with no more than 2 inches of processed bark mulch, an alternative to leaf mold, then waters the tree again for about 10 seconds, or until the water well is filled.

Figure SP-32. To complete the planting process, I snip off any broken or dead branches that resulted from handling the tree from nursery to our garden.

Choosing a Tree in a Garden Center

BAD TREE

GOOD TREE

Figure SP-33. When choosing among trees in plastic containers, push on the trunk of a tree. A good-quality tree will have a strong root system and therefore bend as you push. A poor-quality tree will not bend but give way, because it does not have a solid root system. (After Dr. Ed Gilman)

Bad   **Good**

Figure SP-34. Check the crotches of multistemmed trees to see at what angle, the branches meet the central trunk. The sharper the angle, the weaker the joint and the more likely the branch will break off over time. The wider the angle, the stronger the joint and the longer the branch will remain intact. (After Dr. Ed Gilman)

Figure SP-35. When choosing a small specimen of what will become a large tree, look closely at the branching of the trees for sale in a garden center. A good-quality tree (on the left) will have one central leader (trunk) with branches evenly spaced up the trunk. A poor-quality tree will have multiple leaders, each of which is susceptible to breakage over time where branches meet the trunks. (After Dr. Ed Gilman)

What we did is as important as what we did not do. We did not stake the tree, because this area of the garden is not windy and because the soil of the root ball is heavy clay, much like our soil. Had the soil been sandy, I might have driven one 6-foot stake 18 inches or so into the ground next to the root ball and tied the trunk to it with 1- to 2-inch-wide flexible strapping, which is available at garden supply centers.

PLANTING SHRUBS

All plants that are sold balled and burlapped were grown in the ground, then balled and burlapped the preceding fall and mulched in for the winter, or dug in early spring before the buds began to break. The tree shown on page 70 came in a wire basket inside of which was burlap tied tightly to keep the root ball intact during shipping and planting. Large shrubs sometimes come balled and burlapped as well; plant them using the same principles used to plant a small tree.

Because nurseries are busy in early spring, and because balling and burlapping is time-consuming, more and more nurseries are growing shrubs and even small trees in plastic containers. In general, container plants are smaller than balled-and-burlapped ones, but they're a lot easier to plant, and their root systems are more intact, because the nursery doesn't have to dig into the soil, damaging roots in the process, to extricate the plant.

Here's the sequence I follow to plant a shrub grown in a container.

1. Figure SP-36. I eyeball the size of the container, then dig a hole as deep as it is and twice as wide. As you learned in the section on planting trees, the new thinking is to loosen the soil around the perimeter of a hole for a woody plant but not at the bottom of it, so you set the root ball on undisturbed soil.

2. Figure SP-37. Using the main stem as a handle, I lift the shrub out of the container and set it on the ground near the hole. The key to planting any shrub (or perennial) coming out of a container is to loosen the root ball. I use a three-pronged garden scratcher on the sides and bottom of the root ball to loosen any roots. This particular shrub had not become root-bound; that is, the roots still had plenty of room to grow in this container. That is not always the case, so be certain to loosen perimeter roots, especially when shrubs are root-bound.

3. Figure SP-38. (Opposite) I place the shrub in the hole so the top of its root ball is an inch or so above the adjacent grade. Although I might add a bit of compost to the backfill soil, the new thinking is to put back the same soil that you took out when you dug the hole. I backfill about two-thirds of the way, then water the soil well to be sure there are no hidden air pockets. I let the water settle, then add backfill to be flush with the top

of the root ball. I am careful to put no soil atop the root ball, so its surface roots can continue to provide oxygen for the plant. I also do not push down on the soil with my hand to settle it into the hole. Young roots prefer open, fluffy soil. Watering settles the soil to an appropriate density. I then put 2 inches of processed bark mulch on top of the root ball. We keep an eye on watering, but given that we get about 44 inches of rain per year, we may have to water the shrub only during the latter part of July and the first three weeks of August, and then only once a week. Depending on where you live, you may have to water much more regularly.

4. Figure SP-39. Sometimes when you lift a shrub out of its plastic container, you discover that it is root-bound; that is, you

FIGURE SP-39

What We Did in One Garden Area in Spring 2005

In mid-April 2005, we realized that the Brick Walk Garden needed renovation. If your garden suffers from plants that have grown out of bounds or excessively self-seeded, our approach to the situation may be useful to you as well. Our specific plan of attack has proven helpful whenever we have to deal with a garden that has been in place for many years and needs to be brought back into balance. We start by solving the simple, obvious problems and work toward the more complex ones. Although the plants and problems might be different in your garden, the sequence is the same.

1. First we removed or reduced the number of plants that had excessively self-seeded to the point where they were crowding out others and making themselves too important: *Lobelia siphilitica* and *L. s.* 'Alba', pulmonarias, violets, tradescantias, and lady's mantle (*Alchemilla mollis*).

2. Next we assessed large-scale perennials that had grown out of bounds or no longer interested us. We had to decide whether to totally remove the plants or reduce them in size. We decided to remove all of the *Amsonia tabernaemontana* but transplanted a few small divisions to open areas in another garden. We dug up a yellow daylily that had floppy foliage and flower stems and composted it; we replaced it with a new and particularly floriferous yellow daylily that Martin Viette, a daylily expert from Virginia, sent us. We dug up nearly half of three 18-inch-wide crowns of *Miscanthus sinensis* 'Purpurascens' that had spread beyond reasonable limits, and gave the divisions to friends.

3. We assessed shrubs and decided that two purple-leaf sand cherries (*Prunus* × *cistena*) should be transplanted to a more sunny location. Nearby trees had grown over the years, and the sand cherries were suffering from the resulting shade. We moved them and put two *Cotinus coggygria* 'Royal Purple' in their place. We removed and discarded two *Rosa glauca* that had become too leggy.

4. With several shrubs removed and many perennials gone or reduced in size, we looked at what was left. We found that we had a few red-leaved heucheras over here, a few over there. We massed twelve of them next to a yellow-variegated *Hosta*

'Sagae' to create a dramatic contrast between their differing foliage colors. We grouped three *Rodgersia pinnata* next to one another so they contrasted with the more filigreed foliage of *Aruncus dioicus.*

5. Next we transplanted perfectly healthy and satisfying plants that needed new positions for a variety of reasons: we moved three *Rubus cockburnianus*, with their striking white stems, from deep in the bed to closer to the brick path, where they would be more clearly seen; we massed previously scattered low, blue-flowering hardy geraniums under and around them.

6. We looked for shrubs that could be transplanted to this highly visible garden from other places on our property where they might not be seen. Bringing shrubs into this garden would help reduce maintenance. We transplanted *Hydrangea* 'White Dome' from a corner of the Woodland Garden into the foreground of the Brick Walk Garden; we transplanted a yellow-leaved elderberry from a far corner of the Gray Garden to center stage between a newly reduced *Miscanthus sinensis* 'Purpurascens' and a *Rodgersia*

pinnata. We also brought *Amsonia hubrechtii* (as opposed to the rangier *Amsonia tabernaemontana* that we had removed) from the Entry Garden into the Brick Walk Garden and massed it so it could be seen up close while also contrasting well with adjacent plants.

7. Now that we had open spaces in sun, shade, and semishade for new perennials, we filled the gaps with new cultivars, including *Echinacea purpurea* 'Mango Meadowbrite', *Ligularia dentata* 'Britt-Marie Crawford', *Aralia racemosa, Dicentra* (now *Lamprocapnos*) *spectabilis* 'Gold Heart', and *Monarda* 'Jacob Cline'.

8. We leveled the brick path by taking up bricks that had sunk or been heaved up, then added or took away sand and relaid the bricks, using a level to check our work.

9. We reminded ourselves of what our late friend Dymock Maurice, an octogenarian gardener, had told us about her garden: "It lives at the end of my spade."

see a mass of roots with virtually no soil. To be certain that the roots can extricate themselves from this bound condition, work with the three-pronged scratcher to see if you can loosen the roots. If not, use a handsaw to literally cut into the roots about an inch or less at six points around the perimeter of the root ball; then cut once across the bottom of the root ball. This will cause new feeder rootlets to form, which will venture into the surrounding soil.

PLANTING A NEW HEDGE WHERE OLD SHRUBS WERE

One challenge we all face as we put in gardens and look after them is how to manage them over the long haul. Twenty years ago Mary and I put in a mixed lilac hedge along the west side of our garden to separate the garden from the nearby dirt road (see Figure SP-40). We chose lilacs interplanted with a few other shrubs because there were already several lilacs growing under the mature maple in this photograph. As time passed the maple grew, shading more and more of the lilac hedge, and the lilacs began to lean east for more sun. In winter and early spring, when Richard Brown took this photo, the whole area was a mess.

Mary and I, just like you, have to make tough decisions now and again regarding plants that have been in our gardens for years. Just because they have been there for a long time does not mean they should stay. We decided to remove the lilacs and, because we have a minimal deer problem, plant a yew hedge, which would form a dense evergreen screen between us and the road and provide a background for a new perennial garden east of the hedge.

We planted this lilac hedge (see Figure SP-40) twenty years ago when the maple tree was much smaller. Over time the lilacs could not compete and began to backslide, so we decided to remove them.

Rather than remove all the shrubs, we made the kind of distinctions you can make by assessing each shrub in your garden. We made these distinctions, then asked my colleague Torben Larsen—owner of Windham Growers, here in our village—to come with three of his men and his backhoe. We purposely timed this work months in advance so we would be able to transplant deciduous shrubs before their buds began to open.

1. We left three tree lilacs (*Syringa reticulata*) that were healthy and were far enough away from the shade of the mature maple that they were not leaning.
2. We removed three *Potentilla fruticosa* that were simply beyond the pale; they went on the burn pile across the road.
3. Torben dug up three *Hydrangea paniculata* (see Figure SP-41), and we transplanted them. You'll see where later in this chapter.
4. With the backhoe and front loader, we dug up a 10-foot-high *Syringa vulgaris* 'Sensation' that was in good shape and transplanted it elsewhere in the garden.
5. Many of the lilacs were too misshapen to

FIGURE SP-40

FIGURE SP-41

keep, so they, along with a yellow-leaved ninebark (*Physocarpus opulifolius* 'Dart's Gold'), also went on the burn pile. Given that we love this plant, we purchased three new 'Dart's Gold' and put them in sunnier parts of the garden.

Once all the shrubs were dealt with, Torben used his backhoe to dig a trench about 100 feet long and about 16 inches deep (see Figure SP-42)—about the height of the containers of the yews we had purchased (fifty *Taxus × media* 'Hicksii'). As Torben got closer to the trunk of the mature maple, he made his trench shallower, so we didn't do any more damage to the roots of the maple than was absolutely necessary. When we did sever roots, we were sure to cut off the damaged ends with pruning shears so the root

FIGURE SP-43

FIGURE SP-44

FIGURE SP-45

1. Figure SP-42. I measured the full length of the trench, then divided it by the number of plants we had. I determined that the base of the yews should be 20 inches apart.

2. Figure SP-43. Rather than take that measurement every time we planted a yew, I cut a 20-inch piece from a bamboo stake that we could use to determine a uniform distance between shrubs.

3. Figure SP-44. Because we had kept up an edge along the east side of the old shrub-lilac border, I also cut a

bamboo stake to the appropriate length so we could easily measure how far back from the edge each plant should go. By using these two lengths of bamboo, we were able to create a straight hedge with a uniform distance between shrubs.

4. Figure SP-45. We started planting at the far end of the hedge and worked our way north toward the large maple. We removed several shrubs from their containers at a time and, using a three-pronged garden scratcher, roughed up the perimeter and bottom of each root ball.

5. Figure SP-46. We set each plant in its position, then backfilled only with the soil that had resulted from the trenching, being careful to never get any soil atop the root ball itself. We did not add any compost or soil amendments to the backfill soil. Improving the soil would only make the hedge grow more luxuriantly, and that would add to the number of times I would have to trim the hedge. Yews are strong growers anyway—just look at those roots.

6. Figure SP-47. As we got closer to the maple tree, I planted the shrubs a bit higher, so as not to damage major roots of this important tree. As I planted, Robin came along behind cleaning up. Three of us dug the trench, planted the hedge, watered it in, and cleaned up in about six hours.

FIGURE SP-46

FIGURE SP-47

tips could heal. We hand-dug most of the holes near the maple. Once the trench and holes were dug, I followed this sequence to install the new hedge.

REMOVING OLD SHRUBS

Twice a year—just after the perennials have been cut back in late October, and in early April before they have emerged—I walk through the garden looking just at deciduous and evergreen shrubs. I want to see what shape they're in without having to take their measure in the midst of perennials that grow near or under them. I also want to look them over with an eye to how they're being affected by maturing trees above and perennials below them. This past spring I was walking around the garden thinking just about shrubs and came upon two late lilacs (*Syringa villosa*) growing just to the right of a Columbian urn on the west side of the Brick Walk Garden (see Figure SP-48). When Mary and I planted these lilacs fifteen years earlier, they were upright, well-formed shrubs, and for many years remained upright because the trees just west of them still allowed sun to reach them until around two in the afternoon. But as the years passed the trees grew and threw shade onto the two lilacs by noon at the latest. I had cut down one of the maples to provide more sun for them, but it still wasn't enough. Both lilacs were leaning to the east and looking decidedly uncomfortable. They were also blocking a view down into the Woodland Garden,

Figure SP-48. Once or twice a year, go through your garden to assess shrubs. When I was doing just that in early April, I found that two late lilacs (*Syringa villosa*) to the right of the urn that needed to be removed because they had stopped blooming.

Figure SP-49. I cut down the two late lilacs. Now and again you simply have to make these hard decisions.

Figure SP-50. You don't have to do all the heavy lifting in your garden. Write down a list of jobs well ahead of time, then hire a small backhoe for a day. It is well worth the cost.

and narrowing the entrance to the pea-stone path.

Knowing that Torben would be along in a week or so with his backhoe, I decided to remove these two large shrubs. I got out my chain saw

CALL DIG SAFE

If you plan to dig deeply into the ground with any piece of equipment beyond hand tools, you run the risk of damaging underground utilities. And the list of utility lines has grown immeasurably during the last two to three decades: cables for electricity, telephone, television, computers, satellite communications, alarms, and lighting, and pipes for potable or reclaimed water, sewer, irrigation, natural gas, and oil or steam. In some new communities, as many as fifteen different utility lines can serve a single home, and not all of them have necessarily been installed according to code, so they may not be where they are supposed to be.

At least two to four days before excavating with heavy equipment for such projects as a new patio, the footings for a garden shed, or planting trees along the sidewalk, either you, your landscaper, or the operator of the heavy equipment is required by many states to contact the nationwide organization called Dig Safe. You can get the number for your state by looking in the Yellow Pages of your phone book, by going to digsafe.com on the Internet, or, if you have a cellular phone, dialing 344, which will automatically connect you with your state Dig Safe center. This corporation, supported by the utilities and serving as a liaison between homeowners, contractors, and utility companies, acts at no cost to you or the excavating company working for you. Given that the landscaper or excavating company you hire is more conversant with the work, the depth to which digging will be necessary, and the equipment required to do the job, it is best to ask them to make the call.

Once Dig Safe has been contacted, a company representative will ask the excavator to mark out the limits of the proposed excavation area with white flagging or spray paint. With computer access to utility information, Dig Safe representatives call up your property on their computers to determine what utility lines exist from the street into your home. They then ask the appropriate utility companies to go to your home and mark on the ground with spray paint or colored flags where their underground utility lines run. Each type of utility nationwide has been assigned a certain color with which to mark their lines: green for municipal sewers and drains; purple for reclaimed water and irrigation; blue for potable water; orange for cables related to communications and alarms; yellow for gas, oil, steam, or petroleum products; red for electrical lines, cables, and conduits. Once all the lines are marked, you should photograph them for later reference.

If you fail to call Dig Safe and the work that you or your landscaper authorized results in damage to utility lines, or personal injury to the operator of the heavy equip-

ment, you or your contractor is liable for damages. Go to digsafe.com on the Web to read about the state laws that define your responsibilities and liability regarding utility lines that service your home.

A Dig Safe representative told me that there is no end to the hair-raising stories of people who dug without Dig Safe's knowledge. Severing dangerous power lines, for example, can seriously injure equipment operators and cut power to whole communities for hours or days. To give you an indication of the importance of this process, during the primary construction months from March through November, residents of five New England states (not counting Connecticut) make an average of 15,000 requests a week to the regional Dig Safe center to mark out utility lines.

Carrying out your own initial investigation is also helpful, especially if you have invisible dog fencing, irrigation lines, or your own septic system or artesian well, none of which would be recorded by any utility company. Here's how. First, go to any files you might have on your home and the location of its utility lines. Architectural drawings, septic system installation maps, or what builders call "as-built plans" often show the location of permanent lines.

Next, look in your basement for clues as to where utility lines come through the wall. Knowing where the main septic line enters, for example, will help you determine the rough location of the septic tank; and its position relative to the top of the basement wall will suggest the depth at which the septic line is buried. Look outside for the septic tank vent to help locate the pump chamber. A straight line between the vent and where the septic line enters the basement wall will help you approximate where the septic tank and septic lines are.

Then look for the pressure tank for your water system. Following the 2-inch-thick black plastic line from it as it passes through a hole in the basement wall will help you find the water line and the depth at which it is buried. Look outside for the metal wellhead. Connect the dots and you have a good sense of where water lines are buried.

Check to see if the power line comes into the basement through an underground conduit; if it does, how far down it is from the top of the basement wall suggests how deeply it is buried between the utility pole and your house. Also check your garage and all outbuildings for clues regarding the origin and direction of water and electrical lines. Look for lampposts and even heated birdbaths and their associated electrical lines for clues as to the location of the coaxial cable that runs from your satellite dish to where it runs into your house. Map out where invisible dog fencing is located as well as irrigation lines and sprinkler heads. All of

this information has a great deal to do with how you will develop your garden you don't damage the utility lines that keep your house functioning.

As you locate existing utility lines, or have new ones installed, be sure to keep a record of their exact locations—with measurements on sketches or scaled drawings. And as new utility lines are buried, take photographs that will enable you to remember just where the lines are years later.

Questions to Ask Yourself

- Who should call Dig Safe? Me? My excavator? The landscaper? When?
- To avoid costly liability issues if anything goes wrong during excavation, how do I make certain that the right people made the right phone calls?
- What is the best method I should use to record all the information I gather from Dig Safe's findings, as well as my own initial investigation?
- How and where do I store the information for easy retrieval later?
- Are all subsidiary electrical wires, such as those to garden lighting, not recorded by the Dig Safe people protected by conduit so I don't sever the lines with my shovel?

Figure SP-51. Torben and Mike transplanted the three hydrangeas you see in SP-41 in about forty-five minutes.

Figure SP-52. In about twenty minutes, Siena moved this small shrub with her shovel. Note the dam she installed around the perimeter of the root ball to hold water.

(see Figure SP-49) and cut them down, leaving a stump so Torben would have a point of purchase with his backhoe (see Figure SP-50). To remove the stump, he reached around the back of the shrub, drove his backhoe teeth into the ground, then lifted the root system and stump out of the ground for removal to the burn pile. He used the same approach when lifting three hydrangea shrubs that we transplanted (see Figure SP-41).

TRANSPLANTING SHRUBS

Even before the walkabout to assess all our shrubs, Mary and I had decided to remove the 100-foot-long shrub border (see Figure SP-40) to make way for a new yew hedge. In assessing the shrubs in that area, we decided to transplant the three *Hydrangea paniculata* rather than discard them. Torben reached around the back of each one with his backhoe and lifted them out; we immediately covered their root balls with soil to keep their roots from drying out until he and his helper, Mike, could plant them as a group of three that afternoon.

At another point in my shrub assessment, I came upon a *Hydrangea paniculata* 'White Dome' that I had planted in the Woodland Garden. I had given it a year to settle in, but it clearly was not happy competing for light and nutrients under the mature maple trees. During our day of shrub transplanting, Siena took her shovel and, holding the handle upright, drove the blade into the ground in a 10-inch radius around this small shrub. Had she held her shovel handle at an angle, she would have cut into the root system. She then simply lifted the shrub out of the ground, put it in a wheelbarrow, and replanted it in the midst of the sunnier Brick Walk Garden (see Figure SP-52), where we all felt it would be happier.

Planting Perennials and Annuals

◼ PLANTING PERENNIALS

The key to successfully planting perennials is soil preparation. When we plant an area in perennials, we clear it of weeds, then cover the whole area with as much as 6 inches of well-composted cow manure, leaf mold, or compost and dig it at least a foot into the ground with a spading fork. Once we plant the area, we might mulch with more composted manure or leaf mold. Although

1. Figure SP-53. Siena dug a hole at least twice as wide and deep as the pot the perennial came in. She backfilled the hole with a half-and-half mixture of compost we have made over the years and the topsoil she removed when digging the hole.

3. Figure SP-55. She placed the perennial in the hole so the top of the root ball was flush with the grade of the nearby lawn. She backfilled the hole to within 3 inches of the top with the same soil/compost mix, but stopped backfilling about 3 inches before she reached the top of the hole in preparation for watering.

2. Figure SP-54. She removed the perennial from its pot and with her fingers gently roughed up the bottom and sides of the soil in which the perennial was potted, thereby breaking a kind of seal that forms around the perimeter of the pot. In a way she released the roots so that when set into compost-enriched soil, they readily take hold.

4. Figure SP-56. Because she didn't backfill to the top of the hole, the water did not run off but settled deep into the hole. Having watered, she backfilled with more soil/compost mix even with the top of the root ball, being careful not to add any soil on top of it. She then watered with a second bucketful to be certain that all the soil was moist; water also helps settle the soil close to the entire surface of the root ball, filling in any air pockets that might have formed.

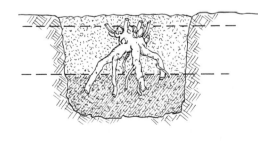

PLANTING PEONY

E. Sears

5. Figure SP-57. Peonies require special treatment. If you plant according to this diagram, your peonies will perform well for years. Howard Andros, my late septuagenarian mentor, told me that the traditional way to plant peonies requires a hole 3 feet deep and across. Never top-dress a peony with animal-based compost, because it will encourage botrytis, a wilting fungus; use leaf mold instead.

we don't add compost or other amendments to the soil when planting trees, and might add just a bit of compost to the soil when planting small shrubs, we amend soil heavily for perennials.

When planting a single perennial (see Figures SP-53 to SP-56), we do the same thing on a smaller scale.

PLANTING ANNUALS IN POTS

Once the garden is cleaned up in the spring, I bring the pots planted with tulips up from the cellar. And I use my ball cart to put some of our terra-cotta pots into place in the garden, even though we won't plant them until Memorial Day (see Figure SP-58). Handsome pots look good in the garden even when they're empty.

As the tulips finish blooming, we uproot them, keeping their foliage intact, and transplant them into Mary's cutting garden across the road. Over time, mice and voles cause the planted tulips to decline, but because we pot up new ones annually, we have lots of cut tulips for the house every spring. We spread the soilless mix from the tulip pots into the garden.

The week before Memorial Day, when we are reasonably certain that there will be no more frosts, we plant annuals in the pots that held tulips. We plant around thirty pots of various sizes and set them throughout the garden: at the ends of beds or hedges; around the entrance to the barn and house; on either side of the broad steps through the Entry Garden. We rely on plants that bloom freely throughout the summer without deadheading, and plants with interesting foliage color and contrast.

Figure SP-58. A ball cart is a very useful tool to have when moving heavy objects throughout the garden.

1. Figure SP-59. We use a soilless planting medium called Pro-Mix, a combination of peat moss, perlite, vermiculite, and fertilizer. To open the 4-cubic-foot bale, I cut it in half with a pruning saw, to make the weight more manageable.

2. Figure SP-60. We lay out the annuals we intend for a specific pot on a tarp along with the pot and soilless mix. This eases cleanup. We then put three or four 2-quart plastic pots upside down in the bottom of the terra-cotta pot to improve drainage and reduce the amount of mixture we need to fill the big pot. Next we fill the terra-cotta pot to within 2 inches or so of the top. Sometimes we add water-absorbent granules (one product name is Soil Moist) to the Pro-Mix to reduce the amount of watering we'll have to do; we mix that into the soilless mix, following directions throughly.

3. Figure SP-61. Next we decide how we'll combine the plants in the pot. Given that we rely on foliage as well as flower color, we hold the plants next to one another to see how compatible the foliage colors and textures are.

4. Figure SP-62. We remove the annuals from their pots and gently loosen their root systems with our fingers so they'll be able to take in nutrients immediately.

FIGURE SP-63

FIGURE SP-65

5. Figure SP-63. We judge the planting depth so that the top of the soilless mix will be about 2 inches below the rim of the pot. This makes watering easier than if we had brought the level right up to the rim, which causes the water to run off.

6. Figure SP-64. (Opposite) We place the pot in its final position (in this case, on its pedestal), then water it with a watering wand fixture at the end of a hose. This saves having to carry a heavy pot to its final destination.

7. Figure SP-65. From early June until late August, we feed the pots weekly with a water-soluble plant food (20-20-20) at the rate of one teaspoon per gallon.

8. Figure SP-66. Mixing the plant food in a watering can ensures the correct proportions. With large plants that are heavy feeders, we also top-dress the soilless mix just after planting with a slow-release pelletized fertilizer such as Osmacote.

FIGURE SP-66

FIGURE SP-68

9. Figure SP-67. (Opposite) *Coleus* (now *Solenostemun*) 'Alabama Sunset', near an entrance to the herb garden, shows the results of planting in a good soilless mix and regular fertilizing.

10. Figure SP-68. *Hibiscus acetosella* 'Maple Sugar' takes advantage of the support provided by the side of the barn.

MULCHES

We use organic mulches, which are derived from plants or manures, because they retain moisture in the soil while helping control weeds, erosion, and muddy backsplash onto the leaves, flowers, fruits, or vegetables. Mulches maintain an even soil temperature winter and summer, thereby encouraging beneficial microorganisms and bacteria and reducing the stress of temperature fluctuation on plants. As mulch decays over time, earthworms incorporate it into the soil, thereby adding organic matter and building up what is called tilth or soil structure, which is especially important in organically starved gravelly, sandy, or clay soils. Mulches also make our garden look good by providing a uniform and unifying color on the ground.

Whenever possible, we use mulches from our area; you should do the same. Here in New England we use white pine needles, shredded leaves from our trees and shrubs, processed bark mulch (see Figure SP-31 on page 75), and lawn clippings. Mulching is simply following nature's cue; if we didn't rake leaves or cut back perennials in autumn, woody and herbaceous plants would mulch themselves with their own leaves.

TIME OF APPLICATION

We apply mulch to existing gardens in late spring, after we've raked all the leaves off the

DIVIDING SNOWDROPS

The best time to divide snowdrops is when they are in bloom—in early April in Vermont. Dividing snowdrops is a simple process that enables you to introduce this delicate spring-blooming bulb into other parts of your garden without spending a cent.

FIGURE SP-70

Figure SP-69. Snowdrops growing at the base of a south-facing stone near our front door bloom several days ahead of those that are just across the driveway on the north side of a weeping larch. The heat of the sun that is absorbed by the stone and released at night awakens these bulbs earlier than those in shady areas of our garden. I dig up the snowdrops with a small garden spade, driving the blade straight into the ground and a few inches from the clump to avoid severing bulbs or stems.

Figure SP-70. To be able to plant individual bulbs, I gently pulled apart the clump and lined them up neatly on the stone for immediate transplanting.

Figure SP-71. One year I took half a shovelful of bulbs and didn't even divide them but simply put the entire division in a hole I had dug under the weeping larch. We got a good show immediately.

FIGURE SP-72

Figure SP-72. I dug lots of compost into a shady area of the garden and planted the snowdrops individually.

Figure SP-73. A couple of years later that approach has resulted in a more naturalized look than when simply transplanting clumps of bulbs.

FIGURE SP-73

Top-dressing with Compost

After raking leaves from the perennial beds, we do our best to spread them with wheelbarrow load after load of well-composted cow manure, leaf mold, or aged compost. Some years we don't have the time to get very far; other years we get a lot done. Having spread the compost about 2 inches thick over the garden, we simply leave it. We don't fork or shovel it in, so as not to damage the surface roots of perennials, shrubs, and small trees. We simply spread the compost on the surface of the beds, and earthworms take it down into the ground. (See Figure SP-74, Figure SP-81 on page 106, and Figure SU-50 on page 142.)

FIGURE SP-74

beds The wetness of heavy rains or melting snow has had a chance to dry out a bit, and the soil has warmed up. Mulch too early and we trap too much moisture in the soil, which therefore stays cold and sodden. We also apply mulch to newly planted perennials, shrubs, trees, or vegetables immediately after planting, whenever that might be—spring, summer, or fall.

We apply about a 2-inch layer of mulch around new plantings. Use less and the mulch would neither hold moisture nor prevent weeds; using more could prevent oxygen from reaching surface roots, and create waterlogged soil. One exception to the rule is to mulch more heavily when planting in fall, then pull all but 2 inches of the mulch away in spring. We keep mulch 3 to 6 inches away from the trunks of trees, the stems of shrubs, and the base of perennials, vegetables, and annuals to allow for air circulation around the base of the plants.

Here are the mulches we use; they are generally available across North America.

Processed Bark Mulch

Because there is a firewood production mill within 15 miles of us that produces vast quantities of inexpensive finely ground bark mulch, we use a lot of it. We spread bark mulch 2 inches thick under shrubs and in a 2- to 3-foot radius around established trees in the lawn. We also use mulch to form paths through the Woodland

Garden, where its use feels appropriate. We replenish this mulch every year; when it decomposes sufficiently, we spread the compost into adjacent beds and start all over again with a fresh layer on the paths.

Avoid adding fresh mulch over decomposed mulch year after year. You'll end up with what is known as "volcano mulching"—tall, cone-shaped piles of mulch that hold undue moisture against the trunks and stems of trees and shrubs and rob surface roots near the trunk of valuable oxygen. Every other year at the very least, remove the aged mulch and dig it into beds or scatter it on your compost pile.

SAWDUST

Sawdust is a long-lasting compost that we have found suitable under blueberries, raspberries, and gooseberries. Once dry, it forms a weed-defeating crust on top that, unlike peat moss, remains porous. As with all wood-based mulches, sawdust has a high carbon content. The microorganisms that break down wood require nitrogen, which has to come from the soil in which plants grow. However, wood-based mulches spread only on the surface draw negligible amounts of nitrogen from the soil. We don't fork sawdust into the soil, because it would draw significant amounts of nitrogen away from our plants. Earthworms do the mixing.

SHREDDED LEAVES

Because whole leaves form a dense, wet mat over the winter, we don't use them in perennial bor-

ders, where they can cause plant crowns to rot. We pile leaves downwind of the garden and allow them to compost themselves over a year's time. The result is rich, porous, organic leaf mold, which plants love. We spread it 3 to 4 inches thick on the soil around perennials in spring.

PINE NEEDLES

If we can find pine needles when we need them, we mulch recently planted or transplanted perennials with 2 to 3 inches of the needles to help conserve moisture around the root system yet allow air to circulate among the needles. After a few months we remove the needles before they have had time to decompose and acidify the soil. Pine needles are also the perfect mulch for all acid-loving broad-leaved and needled evergreens. Though we have not gone to the effort of laying down pine boughs in late fall, many gardeners in our area do, because they make a superb winter mulch for perennial beds. They lay the boughs onto beds after the top 2 inches of soil is frozen, and leave them on until early spring. The purpose is to keep the soil reliably and uniformly frozen throughout the winter. This helps reduce heaving of the crowns of perennials from the freeze-thaw cycle.

STRAW AND HAY

Baled straw is made up of the dried, nearly grain-less stems of barley, oats, or wheat, whereas hay

FIGURE SP-75

FIGURE SP-76

FIGURE SP-77

ARRIVAL OF A DELIVERY TRUCK

In preparation for spring, Mary and I sit down most winters to develop an order for trees and shrubs for spring planting. We don't do this every year by any means, but this past year we ordered enough to justify having the plants delivered rather than my going for them in my pickup truck. Here's the delivery from a nursery that supports gardening professionals.

1. Figure SP-75. Even before trees and shrubs at a nursery yard are loaded, they are tied with stout twine so their branches are held tight to the trunk to prevent limb breakage. Plants that have a tight form anyway, or are small enough not to require it, are not tied. All the plants are then carefully loaded onto the truck and covered with a heavy tarp to

FIGURE SP-78   FIGURE SP-79   FIGURE SP-80

prevent windburn during the drive from nursery yard to us.

2. Figure SP-76. Knowing a couple of weeks ahead which day this delivery was due, I asked Torben Larsen to come with three men and his backhoe to help us off-load, then stay on for the day to help us plant. Mary and I would plant whatever was left. Having this manpower makes for an efficient day. As each plant comes off the truck, I show the guys where it will be planted. We use a ball cart to move large shrubs. Smaller ones go in a wheelbarrow.

3. Figure SP-77. By the time we have unloaded the truck, every plant has been taken to a spot close to where it will be planted. Here are two dogwoods (*Cornus sanguinea* 'Winter Flame'), which we'll plant in front of the arborvitae hedge so that all year long the dogwood's brightly colored stems will show up against the dark green background. We'll cut the strings before planting so we can determine the dogwood's best side. We'll

remove the burlap and wire basket from the root ball once the ball is in the planting hole.

4. Figure SP-78. Greg Hunt and Torben roll all the heavy shrubs and trees into the front loader of the backhoe. (You have to love hydraulics.) Notice that they pad the trunks of the trees so the tender bark is not damaged as it rubs against the metal front loader. (The tender bark of a tree is easily damaged.)

5. Figure SP-79. Torben drives the backhoe right to the trees' future spots in the garden rather than just setting them on the driveway. This adds a few more minutes to the unloading process, but in the end we have handled each tree only once (these are *Amelanchier* × *grandiflora* 'Autumn Brilliance').

6. Figure SP-80. We use the little trailer attached to my lawn tractor to deliver smaller shrubs such as the *Taxus* × *media* 'Hicksii' that will become part of the hedge.

is made up of dried grasses and often weeds growing in hayfields. Straw is weed free, whereas baled hay is riddled with hay and weed seeds. Because straw includes stouter stems than those of hay, it stacks much like jackstraws, so air and water can pass through it easily. We use straw under tomatoes, strawberries, and many vegetables that ripen near the surface of the soil and would be damaged by soil splashing onto them during rain or irrigation. Straw or hay is good for mulching paths between rows of vegetables as well as the soil under the vegetables themselves.

LAWN CLIPPINGS

Lawn clippings are rich in nitrogen, so they are best left on the lawn to decompose and rebuild the soil. However, during the spring or other wet periods when the lawn grows 3 inches in three days, clippings build up. We rake the clumps of cut grass immediately after mowing, then compost the clippings or put them under the raspberries, being careful not to lay down more than 3 to 4 inches; more than that and within two to three hours after mowing, fermentation will start and the clippings will sour. A thin layer of nitrogen-rich lawn clippings is excellent mulch for vegetables but not perennials. Because we don't use any chemicals on our lawn, or anywhere else in the garden, we use the clippings without being concerned that chemicals will find their way into our fruits and vegetables.

COCOA-BEAN AND BUCKWHEAT HULLS

We tried cocoa-bean and buckwheat hulls several years ago, but found them unsatisfactory for overall garden use in this area of the country, which gets 44 inches of rain a year. We found that 2 inches of these mulches were most appropriate in small rose, herb, or perennial beds, or for covering the soil in pots planted with annuals. The problems with cocoa hulls are that when dry they are easily blown about, that after the first rain they mat together, and that if they stay wet for even two or three days, an unsightly white mold forms atop large mats of the hulls (a problem in wet areas of the country). Buckwheat hulls are preferable, but given the cost and the fact that both products last only one season, we have given up using them.

FIGURE SP-81

CHECKLISTS

EARLY SPRING

- Clean up the garden shed.
- Organize tools so they are accessible.
- Sort through your tools to select those that are taking up valuable space but you never, or rarely, use. Store them out of the way.
- Pressure-check hoses for leaks.
- Check new lists of invasive plants to see which you may have to remove.
- Cut back invasive shrubs such as barberry in preparation for their removal when the ground thaws.
- As the snow melts, stand on adjacent lawn to rake wet, matted leaves from the edges of beds; don't walk into the beds until the soil has dried out a bit.
- Pick up sticks from the lawn, gather them on a tarp, and use bundles of these dried sticks to start a fire to burn the brush pile.
- Rake the lawn and put material raked up on the compost pile.
- Divide snowdrops when they are in bloom.

LATE SPRING

- Cut new edges along gardens that meet lawn.
- Rake leaves off gardens before plant growth begins. Avoid doing this too soon, so the emerging tender tips don't get frostbitten. Use care around bulbs coming up. If neces-sary, clean leaves off the surface of the ground around emerging plants by hand.
- Cut back ornamental grasses and other herbaceous plants left up for winter interest.
- Cut back woody perennials such as *Perovskia atriplicifolia* to about 12 inches.
- Prune fruit trees in March.
- Sharpen tools, including shovels, pruning shears, and lopping shears.
- Assess your tools, and order replacements if needed.
- In late spring, once any remaining dead leaves have stopped blowing around your garden, clean by hand those wedged in twiggy shrubs.
- Uproot perennial weeds such as dandelions by hand even before new growth tips on perennials have begun to break the soil sur-face. Such perennial weeds are obvious at that point in the year. Don't use a hoe; you don't know what growing shoots lay below the ground that you might damage.
- Once dead leaves have stopped blowing around your garden, top-dress the garden with leaf mold or compost.
- Assess all the walking surfaces and built structures in the garden for winter damage, and make necessary repairs.
- Top-dress pea-stone, gravel, bark mulch, or any other loose-surfaced paths.
- Check stone or brick paths and terraces for heaving and sinking caused by winter freeze-thaw cycles; you may have to level some sur-faces.
- Once the soil has dried out enough to be

workable, take divisions of herbaceous perennials.

- Transplant deciduous shrubs before their buds break and the leaves begin to emerge.
- Transplant evergreen shrubs anytime before new growth appears.
- Buy plants such as pansies that will take some frost, so you'll have early blooming plants for pots or beds.
- Look through the whole garden to see if you missed cutting back any perennials last fall. Cut them back now before new growth starts.
- Clean out pools and ponds and their water filters.
- Straighten out any posts that are leaning after being pushed around by frost in the ground.
- Remove excess self-seeded herbaceous plants such as *Lobelia siphilitica* that have come through the winter with evergreen crowns. They show up in multitudes in early spring like little bright green beacons.
- Group and rearrange plants.
- If you have outdoor lighting, check that all the bulbs are intact, the fixtures firmly in place and safely wired. Clean the fixtures. Be sure that wiring is out of sight.
- Move stored pots, outdoor furniture, ornaments, and gates back into their places in the garden.
- Prune browning branches and twigs on evergreens such as junipers, arborvitae, and yew, and broad-leaved evergreens such as rhododendrons.
- Cut back graying older stems on red-, yel-low-, or green-stemmed dogwoods to bring on new, bright growth.
- Tie up vines whose supports were damaged during the winter.
- Prune maples and other trees that bleed when sawn or pruned after the trees have leafed out.
- Wait until late May or June to shear evergreen hedges, such as yew or boxwood.
- Avoid using electric hedge shears to prune your shrubs into buns. They make it too easy to create unattractive uniform shapes.

WHAT TO DO WITH LEFTOVER SOD

- **Fill in gaps or damaged areas in existing lawn.**
- **Repair worn areas of lawn in a path.**
- **Simplify edges of beds by patching in sod where niggling edges now exist.**
- **Remove rocks from your lawn, backfill the resulting holes with topsoil, and patch with sod.**
- **Replace tiny insignificant island beds with sod.**
- **Backfill low spots in your lawn with soil, then patch them with sod.**
- **Lay leftover scraps of sod upside down on your compost pile so they don't take root.**

Installing and Maintaining a Sod Lawn

Sod is sold by the square foot. A typical pallet delivered directly from a sod farm holds about 500 square feet; if you order from a garden center or nursery, you'll likely be able to order any number of square feet. Measure the area you want to sod to get a square-foot figure, then order that amount plus 20 percent more. There is inevitable waste as you cut sod to form it around trees and along stone walls and bed edges.

Measuring the square footage of sod in a square or rectangular area is easy: multiply length times width. If the area curves in and out, get help in calculating your square-foot order by going to www.super sod.com, the Patten Seed Company Web site, then click on "Laying sod," then go to their "Yard Area Calculator" section. Sod only those parts of your garden that get at least six to seven hours of direct sun a day, and choose a grass type that is right for your area of the country. Virginia bluegrass is not right for everyone, though it sure looks good here in the Northeast.

Seeding versus Sodding

- TIMING: You can install sod anytime from early spring until two to three weeks before the ground freezes. Here in Vermont, seeding a lawn is most successful in the narrow time frame from late August to early September, when fewer crabgrass seeds germinate but all lawn seed will germinate.

- COST: Measure cost in terms of money and time. Sod costs more at the outset but involves much less work overall. There is none of the fuss and bother that comes with seeding: having to weed out the huge number of weed seeds already in your soil that germinate with the grass seed; keeping the mulch straw in place on windy days; and keeping the area evenly watered, and having to walk on the muddy spots after watering. The list goes on.

- SEED LARGE AREAS; SOD SMALL AREAS: If you have to seed a large area, hire someone. Professionals prepare the soil with tractor-based equipment, then blow seed and mulch onto the prepared area with a machine called a hydroseeder. The mulch helps retain water and doesn't blow away. For a small area (500 square feet or so), you can lay sod yourself.

- QUALITY OF RESULTS: Laying out a sodded lawn is like magic. Open soil turns to green lawn in a matter of hours. With the correct soil preparation, regular watering, and the recommended mower height, sodded lawns set roots within weeks and quickly provide a useful, attractive surface.

THE SEQUENCE OF LAYING SOD

1. If the area to be covered with sod has poorly growing lawn grass on it, skim it off with a shovel, then rototill. Don't try to rototill existing lawn grass into the soil; it will form unmanageable clumps that will create a moundy, lumpy base for the sod.

2. Rototill to a depth of 3 to 4 inches; remove all roots, stones, and other debris.

3. Rake the soil level with a broad steel rake; the wider it is, the better to create a uniform surface on which to lay the sod. Be sure the surrounding grade will drain rainwater away from your house.

4. Do a simple test for pH so you know whether or not to add lime to the soil. In most areas of the country affected by acid rain, you can safely spread 50 pounds of dolomitic lime per 1,000 square feet, and rake it in. In the Midwest and Southwest, where the soil pH is naturally high, you may not want to add any lime at all.

5. Rent a lawn roller, and complete all preparatory work before calling for a sod delivery. Rolls of sod dry out quickly.

6. Sod comes in strips about 18 inches wide and 3 to 4 feet long. The strips are rolled and delivered on pallets. Water down the exterior of all the sod exposed to sunlight. Load several rolls into a wheelbarrow, then cover the remaining rolls with a tarp to shade the exposed roots.

7. Start laying sod immediately after delivery. If you wait even a day, the sod in the interior of the rolls will begin to yellow. After two days, a high percentage of the interior sod will be spoiled.

8. Stretch twine taut between two bamboo stakes to be sure you have a straight line—if that's what you're after—against which to lay the first line of sod. This determines the line that every subsequent sod will follow.

9. Water the soil where you will lay the sod, then lay the first line of sod against the twine.

10. Before laying the second line of sod, look for the seams between the ends of the sod in the first row. Be sure not to line up seams in the second row with those of the previous one. Stagger the ends in all the rows (see Figure SOD-1), in the same way that bricklayers stagger bricks from row to row on a house.

11. Lay all sod tightly to one another along the sides and ends. Leave no gaps.

12. Once you have completed an area, roll it with the lawn roller filled with water—the heavier the roller, the better. You want to be sure that all the undersurfaces of the sod are in direct contact with the underlying soil.

MAINTENANCE OF A SODDED LAWN

1. Watering is the key to successful sodding. Depending on the frequency of rain, water daily for two hours for the first week or so, then every other day for the next three weeks, then every fourth day for the next four weeks, until you are watering once a week for the balance of the first growing season. Set up sprinklers in a predetermined pattern so you're certain that the entire sodded area receives an equal amount of water.

2. After about ten days to two weeks, mow the sod for the first time, and mow high. Set the rotary mower blade at about 3½ to 4 inches off the ground. Keep the mower blade that high for the first season.

3. We laid about 2,000 square feet of sod a few years back, and even as careful as our colleague Torben Larsen and his men were, crabgrass and other weeds began to appear in the second year at the outer edges of the sodded area and in some of the seams between individual sods. Mary weeded the whole area twice the second year, and that has kept the weeds in check.

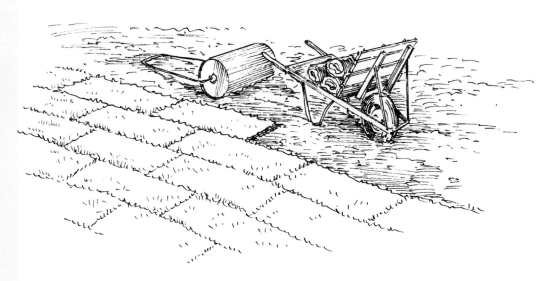

Figure SOD-1. Once you have prepared the soil on which you will lay the sod, roll the ground with a heavy roller. Lay the sod on it, then roll the sod to ensure there is uniform contact between sod and soil. Regular and deep watering is also essential; don't let the sod dry out. Also, set your mower deck at 3–4 inches for the first season.

Summer

Figure SU-1. (Opposite) In the Brick Walk Garden in early June, Siberian iris and *Paeonia* 'Claudia' bloom in the foreground with hardy geraniums; in the background is pink *Rosa glauca*. Notice the pollarded willow in the upper right corner. **Figure SU-2.** This late-summer combination in the Brick Walk Garden includes an ornamental grass (*Miscanthus sinensis* 'Purpurascens'), two annuals (the white *Nicotiana* 'Fragrant Cloud' and the burgundy-leaved Perilla), a yellow daylily, and the terra-cotta-colored *Helenium* 'Moerheim Beauty'. Five-leaved akebia (*Akebia quinata*) grows on the pergola in the background.

SPRING IS FOR PLANTING; SUMMER IS FOR TENDING what we planted. Summer is *the* time of year for what most of us regard as garden maintenance: weeding and staking perennials, mowing the lawn, deadheading flowering perennials, watering and fertilizing annuals in pots. Spring is a rush to get everything done; summer is a time to attend methodically to plants. It's also a time to stand back and enjoy the fruits of our labor.

The relative calm of summer affords us time to appreciate what we have accomplished in spring and over the years in our garden. Virtually every evening of the growing season, Mary and I walk the garden to see what's just come up, what's in bloom, what's just going by. Before we set out on a walk, we sometimes decide whether it will be a walk to assess the garden or simply enjoy it.

Figure SU-3. This is the sitting area at the north end of the Long Borders. *Paeonia* 'Roselette' blooms with *Allium aflatunense* in the foreground in early June. We subsequently removed the invasive *Berberis thunbergii* 'Atropurpurea' to the far left of the photo and replaced it with purple-leaved ninebark (*Physocarpus opulifolius* 'Diabolo').

Figure SU-4. Looking south down the length of the Long Borders in June shows bearded iris in bloom as well as the large white-flowered *Crambe cordifolia* on the right.

We gardeners are tough on ourselves. Every time we walk the garden on our own, rather than with visitors, we often focus on what's wrong with it. Why did I put that plant there? Why didn't I prune out that dead branch? What did we have in mind when we planted that? We berate ourselves, find fault with our garden, and remain on that maddening path toward what we imagine as perfection. Once in a while, that's fine. Clearly we have to take stock of the garden, make work lists, talk with each other about what we'll do on the weekend to improve the garden.

But we all have another need, and that is to simply *be* in the garden. It took a friend to make that point clear to us. Eva Mondon leads what she calls walking meditations now and again during the warm months of the year. Many summers ago Eva called to ask if she could lead one of her walks in our garden. We were happy she asked, and a few days later, on a Sunday morn-

ing, she and about eight others arrived. Mary and I joined in. After a few words about what to expect, Eva rang a small bell, and for the next hour or so, no one said a word.

She led us to about ten spots in our garden. Upon arriving at each location, she stopped. At first I found myself looking at the garden as I always do—as a lovely place to be, with an eye on that floppy hollyhock I should have staked. I was also aware that I was trying to banish all thought of work.

As we got well into the hour-long walk, however, I realized I was listening in a new way, smelling fragrances in a new way, seeing flowers and plants in a new way. It was moment that was utterly unself-conscious for all of us. Mary and I vowed to repeat this quiet walk, sometimes on our own, sometimes with each other. I urge you to try it sometime. Just walk quietly in your garden and be free of judgment.

Figure SU-5. We combine different foliage colors in the Brick Walk Garden to provide lasting color. Flower color is certainly of interest, but many flowers last only a week or two. Leaves last for seven months.

Figure SU-6. Before: Mary uses a kneeler so she can comfortably get close to her work. She's holding back the leaves of *Hosta* 'Royal Standard' so she can weed right up to its crown.

Figure SU-7. After: Mary has weeded all around the crown of the hosta as well as out to the lawn edge.

Bed Maintenance

WEEDING

Henry David Thoreau defined weeding as the business of "making invidious distinctions with a hoe." Weeding is one of those tasks that can become deeply engaging if you give yourself over to it. The engagement relies on a feeling for detail, on your ability to see clearly and look closely, and on the sentiment that when you are weeding you are making those invidious distinctions between weeds you don't want and flowering perennials you do want. Now, dare I say in this age of political correctness that women are better than men at making these distinctions? I know full well that Mary is far and away better at weeding than I am. She has the patience, the sense of detail, and the necessary level of engagement. While I'm off mowing half an acre of lawn, Mary is weeding, and when she is finished with a bed, it looks terrific. And when I finish mowing the lawn, it looks terrific too.

Before we even get to the act of weeding, there are certain things we do to prevent weeds from taking hold in the first place.

Figure SU-8. A scuffle hoe is especially good for weeding in areas with pea stone that would be too disrupted by a typically bladed hoe.

Figure SU-9. Mary scuffle-hoes an area with pea stone atop landscape fabric, then picks up the weeds by hand.

Figure SU-10. She top-dresses any landscape fabric exposed by the weeding.

Figure SU-11. (Opposite) Narrow paths through small gardens are more easily and efficiently groomed if they're dressed with low-maintenance pea stone rather than high-maintenance lawn.

- We mulch woody shrubs such as rhododendrons and witch hazel with 2 inches of processed bark to deter weeds from growing under them.
- We mass ground covers such as hardy geraniums that will shade the ground under crab apples, for example, preventing sunlight from getting to the surface of the soil so weed seeds don't germinate.
- We plant perennials close to one another.

Like massed ground covers, they throw so much shade onto the ground that few weeds develop.
- We top-dress perennial beds with leaf mold whenever possible, safe in the knowledge that, unlike some of our compost, leaf mold will be free of seeds of weeds as well as freely seeding perennials such as lobelia and feverfew.

When weeds do take hold, Mary has her

weeding rules, many of which might be helpful as you tackle weeds in your own garden.

- Weed for a few hours every few days rather than many hours every other week. Don't let so many weeds build up that you become discouraged.
- Attend to the details and be vigilant; weeding is as much about seeing as it is about work.
- Remove weeds from the garden; don't simply pass a hoe over the soil and leave the dead weeds on the surface.
- Lift plant foliage to weed right up to the crown on all sides. (See Figures SU-6 and SU-7.)
- Weed with your fingers if the weeds are small and in tight spaces.
- After weeding an area, scratch the surface with a three-pronged scratcher to aerate it and remove footprints. Aerating the soil allows the surface to dry out, thereby forming less advantageous conditions for the germination of weed seeds. Scratch out footprints, because they put weed seeds in direct contact with the nurturing soil and enhance their germination.
- Kneel to weed instead of standing up and working with the end of a hoe. Kneeling saves your back, and it allows you to weed under plants more easily and see small weeds more clearly.
- Learn the differences in leaf color and form between weeds and perennials to help you distinguish between the two.

PATH MAINTENANCE

The $\frac{3}{8}$-inch pea stone that we use here and there throughout the garden brings a crunchy, light-colored texture onto the ground and underfoot. In spring, we do our best to rake the leaves and winter debris from these paths, but invariably fine decomposed materials filter into the pea stone. Some of our paths have been in place for more than ten years and still look fine. I attribute that to the fact that we stay on top of leaf raking spring and fall, and that we did not put the pea stone directly onto the ground, or even onto crushed gravel. Wherever we wanted pea stone as a mulch or a path, we dug up 3 inches of sod, put down 2 inches of crushed gravel, covered it with woven black landscape fabric, then spread 1 inch of $\frac{3}{8}$-inch pea stone on top of the fabric. The fabric prevented the pea stone from being forced into the gravel by the soles of our shoes.

That's not to say that weed seeds don't blow into and take hold in the areas we've covered with this loose material. They do, though I have to say that the sunnier the spot, the more weeds take root. Figure SU-8 shows the business end of a scuffle hoe that we use almost exclusively to maintain our pea-stone and gravel paths. Having sharpened the blade, we pass it just under the surface of the pea stone, and it severs the weed top and crown from its roots (see Figure SU-9). Mary then rakes up the weeds and puts them in her bucket. Now and again she'll get half a wheelbarrow load of extra pea stone that we have stored across the road, and with a shovel (see Figure SU-10) she top-dresses the recently weeded area to cover any cloth exposed during weeding.

Figure SU-12. Weeding around stepping-stones in a path keeps the path visible.

Figure SU-13. Mary tosses weeds into a bucket, then periodically empties the bucket into a nearby wheelbarrow. A bucket is closer to ground level than is the pan of a wheelbarrow, so the tossing takes less effort.

We also have pea-stone paths in the Herb Garden. There is a good maintenance story in Figure SU-11 that you should take to heart if you have lawn paths in small garden areas. About twenty years ago we put in the four quadrants of our herb garden by simply cutting four rectangles out of a panel of lawn between the hedges you see in Figure W-2 on page 20. By default we created narrow lawn paths around all sides of these four beds. I soon discovered the folly of leaving the lawn in the form of paths. I spent hours and hours edging the little lawn paths so the grass wouldn't migrate into the beds. Finally, in desperation, I measured the total linear feet of the edging for this roughly 30-square-foot garden. I found I was tending 192 linear feet of lawn edge.

I got to work with my straight-nosed spade. I lifted every square inch of those lawn paths by taking up the sod and a couple of inches of top-soil in which the grass was growing. I put soil and sod into the wheelbarrow and hauled it all to the compost pile or filled in dips in the lawn. I wheelbarrowed back enough crushed gravel to cover the paths with a 2-inch-thick layer. I topped that with 1 inch of pea stone. What you see in Figure SU-11 has been intact now for more than ten years. Only recently have we had to scuffle-hoe the paths once a summer, but that's a whole lot less work than the lawn paths required.

WEEDING BETWEEN STEPPING-STONES

For fine weeding, Mary uses a kneeler so she is close to her work (see Figure SU-13). Rather than using a hoe with a 4- to 5-foot-long handle, she uses her favorite weeding tool, a hand hoe with a 6-inch wooden handle, a tempered steel shaft about 10 inches long, and an elongated triangular blade perhaps 5 inches long. Because it comes to a fine point at one end and a slightly blunter end at the other, this tool can get right up to the edge of stepping-stones and even just under their edges, where roots like to gather in soil kept cool and moist by the stones themselves.

As you can see in Figure SU-13, a lot of plants have insinuated themselves into this path. Using

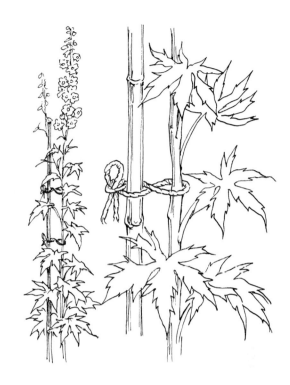

Staking   E Sian

Figure SU-14. Siena has pushed a 4-foot bamboo stake into the ground next to the stem of a hollyhock. She then takes a piece of stout beige or green twine and ties a knot in two or three places up the stem so that in a wind this 6- to 7-foot-high flowering stem will not break.

Figure SU-15. An alternative is to wrap the twine around the flower stem, then twist it once to provide a buffer between the knot and the stake. Then tie the knot to the supporting stake.

the sharp blade of her weeder, Mary removes all the seedlings of many invasive plants that have grown into the spaces between the stepping-stones, but she will leave desirable plants along path edges. We do remove invasive wild violets, which we never can totally eradicate from the garden, as well as lily-of-the-valley. Lovely as its fragrance is in spring, lily-of-the-valley can be a real nuisance, because it spreads easily by roots just under the soil surface. Within a couple of hours, Mary will have this 30-foot-long path weeded.

STAKING

Tall, upright plants such as hollyhock, the flowering stems of *Crambe cordifolia*, Joe Pye weed (*Eupatorium maculatum* 'Gateway'), some ornamental grasses, and a few peonies need staking if we intend to see their flowers. It's a simple task that doesn't take long. The reward? Plants look tended, their stems stay straight, and their blooms stay out of the mud.

Another way to stake plants is to cut small

SUMMER CUTTING BACK OF CERTAIN PERENNIALS

In late June or early July in our Zone 4 garden, many—not all—hardy geraniums need attention. After the first flush of bloom starts to go by in *Geranium oxonianum* 'Claridge Druce', a second burst of fresh new foliage sprouts from the center of the plant. Simultaneously all the foliage on the perimeter flops. The plant will be perfectly fine if we don't cut back the outer ring of floppy foliage, but if we do, we get a second, if less floriferous, bloom in August. Here, Mary (who practices Yoga daily) bends over to cut back the perimeter foliage while leaving the upright inner leaves. (See Figures SU-16, SU-17, and SU-18.)

We grow many different varieties of *Phlox paniculata* because of the range of colors they introduce into the late summer garden. With the exception of 'David', a white-flowering form that is reliably resistant to powdery mildew, most forms of this species are susceptible to powdery mildew. This disease takes hold in the conditions we provide: a dense perennial border with reduced air circulation around and within each plant. To increase air circulation, in early June—or even earlier than we show in these photos—Mary thins each clump of *Phlox paniculata* by removing about a third of the stems at ground level—to try to keep powdery mildew in check. (See Figures SU-19 to SU-21.)

Fall-blooming asters can get so tall that they flop over. To prevent that, and remarkably enough to increase flowering, Mary takes a pair of hedge shears in early June, well before flower buds have formed on asters, and shears back the plants a foot or more to make them denser. (See Figures SU-22 and SU-23.) As you can see in Figure SU-24, there is no lack of blooms two months later.

FIGURE SU-16

FIGURE SU-17

FIGURE SU-18

saplings or branches, then prune them to look like an extended form of your forearm, hand, and five fingers. Choose long branches that have five or so branchlets growing from them. Cut the branch itself to create a sturdy base, then cut off the tips of the branchlets. Push the stout end of the branch into the ground next to the plant you want to support, and set the "finger end" of the branch against the plant. If you surround a floppy plant with several of these homemade supports, the plant will stand far more upright and you will barely know that the supports are there because they often look like they are part of the perennial you're staking.

FIGURE SU-19

FIGURE SU-20

Deadheading Perennials

Perennials are so beautiful, so luxuriant in their bloom, and so rewarding to grow, yet they require attentive maintenance to look their best. If you don't remove spent blooms—that is, if you don't deadhead—herbaceous perennials will look raggedy. When we started developing our garden more than twenty years ago, we planted a lot of herbaceous perennials because we wanted flower and color. Now we are coming to terms with that decision.

We no longer have the same time or energy

Figure SU-21

Figure SU-22

Figure SU-23

we had when we were in our late forties and younger. We have to make a serious decision, and soon. To reduce maintenance, we may have to reduce the number of perennials and increase the number of woody flowering shrubs. But in the meantime, we do have perennials, we keep ordering perennials by the score, and we look after them. Deadheading is one of those chores we keep up with because, as you may have gathered by now, we are *tidy*.

There are several reasons to deadhead.

1. Taking off individual spent blooms improves the look of the plant and keeps it tidy, as with daylilies, bearded and Siberian iris, geum, ajuga, ligularia, goatsbeard (*Aruncus dioicus*), sedum, and sweet cicely.

2. Removing spent blooms or flowering stems encourages the formation of new buds, *Coreopsis verticillata* 'Moon-beam', *Hemerocallis* 'Stellad'Oro', and 'Happy Returns', as with helianthe-

mum, *Leucanthemum superbum* 'Becky', and heuchera.

3. Cutting back 75 to 85 percent of certain flowers and foliage forces a second flush of flowers and foliage later in the season, as with some hardy geraniums, nepeta, and feverfew.

4. Removing flowers and the seed heads that follow flowering prevents excessive self-seeding, as with *Allium aflatunense*, dame's rocket (*Hesperis matronalis*), *Crambe cordifolia*, mallow, teasel, Scotch thistle, echinops, and lady's mantle (*Alchemilla mollis*).

5. Removing seedpods and saving the seeds lets you scatter them later or sow them in trays to produce seedlings, as with *Primula japonica*, hollyhock, digitalis, and *Lobelia syphilitica*.

6. When all the buds on a flowering daylily stem have bloomed, for example, or when the flowers of a hosta have gone by, you can make the plant look

Lawn Mowing

1. Make one pass to throw the mown grass clippings away from a bed.
2. Make a second pass, also throwing the clippings away from the bed or wall.
3. Reverse direction and throw the mown grass clippings toward the beds. If your mower is like mine, the clippings will not reach the beds but be thrown no farther than the edge of the previously mowed lawn. From this point on, direct the clippings away from the area not yet mown, so you don't build up unsightly grass clippings as you move toward the center.

4. Set the mower, so the grass is cut 2 to 4 inches high; I typically leave it $2\frac{1}{4}$ to $2\frac{1}{2}$ inches high. (See Figures SU-25 to SU-27.)

Every November I take my lawn mower to the dealer to have it serviced. They change the oil, sharpen the blades, look over the entire machine, and make whatever repairs will ensure that it works well for another year.

I learned to look after garden machinery from Dr. Oscar Schoenemann, for whom I gardened and mowed lawns when I was a

Figure SU-25

Figure SU-26

teenager. Dr. Schoenemann had five acres of lawn that I mowed every Saturday with his gang Locke lawn mower, which had a central mowing blade and two wing blades. After several hours of mowing, I took the mower to the workshop. With an air compressor hose and nozzle, I blew off any grass clippings still on the machine. I then washed it with soap and water and rinsed it with a hose. Next I dipped fine steel wool in a kerosene/oil mix and cleaned the cutting edges on all three mowing reels. Then I sprayed the entire mower with the kerosene/oil mix, and stored it in the barn for another week.

Every November, Dr. Schoenemann delivered the mower back to the Locke manufacturing plant in Bridgeport, on the coast of Connecticut, to have it checked out, repaired, or reconditioned. After more than twenty-five years of using that machine, he sold it back to the Locke Company as an antique for five times what he paid for it. The company displayed it in their main offices for years.

FIGURE SU-27

neater by reaching well down within the foliage to cut off the entire spent flower stem as near to its base as is practical, instead of simply cutting the spent flower head itself from the top of its stem.

There are times when we do not deadhead spent blooms, because attractive seed heads form after flowers fall; as with peony, astilbe, dictamnus, baptisia, and many alliums, such as 'Globemaster' and *Allium christophii*. These seed heads add interest to the mid- and late-summer garden.

FIGURE SU-31   FIGURE SU-32

We also leave flower heads on certain massed fall-blooming plants, such as ornamental grasses, rudbeckia, and *Sedum* (now *Hylotelephium*) *spectabile*, along with others that die gracefully and go into and through the winter looking reasonably good. Having said that, we leave only masses of these plants intact; if we have just a couple here and there in the garden, there is little reason to leave them.

Here are specifics regarding deadheading some widely grown perennials.

1. Figure SU-28. **Daylilies:** The flower of a daylily blooms for one day. Look closely at this photograph and the other three in this section on daylilies and you'll see that flowers are borne atop single stout stems that hold many buds, only one of which is in full bloom at any one time; the buds yet to bloom are in various stages of maturity. The flowers in these images opened at dawn on the day Richard Brown photographed them; they stayed open for the day, then slowly closed that evening. Here Mary is deadheading the spent blooms from the day before; she's wearing gloves because the "bloom" on these flowers, especially when they're wet, stains her hands.

2. Figure SU-29. Here is a daylily before Mary attended to it. You can see which flowers bloomed the day before, were pollinated, closed up overnight, and are now waiting to mature and fall off.

3. Figure SU-30. Rather than wait for the spent blooms to fall off, Mary picks them off, so the remaining flowers look better.

4. Figure SU-31. Once all the buds on a flowering stem have completed their cycle of forming, blooming, and going by, Mary cuts off the flower stem at its very base. You can see that the top of the spent stem has turned beige, so it has been a week or more since the last flower bloomed on that stem.

FIGURE SU-33   FIGURE SU-34   FIGURE SU-35

Daylilies are one of many plants that hold their flowers atop stout stems as opposed to sending out their flowers along the stems, or from joints where leaf meets stem. Let's look at how we deadhead a number of such perennials that flower atop dedicated flowering stems.

1. Figure SU-32. **Masterwort** (*Astrantia major*): This plant has separate stems for flower and foliage. Once flowers atop the flower stem begin to brown off, we cut the stem at the base to avoid an unsightly brown stem poking out of the green foliage. We cut this back before seeds form, because this is a very freely seeding plant that can become a nuisance if it is not deadheaded promptly after flowering.

2. Figure SU-33. **Bearded iris** (*Iris × germanica*): Once all the buds on a bearded iris have bloomed, we reach down to the very bottom of the flowering stem and cut it off. The energy the plant requires to set seed is far better spent in supporting

foliage and the rhizome on which the entire plant depends.

3. Figure SU-34. **Feverfew** (*Matricaria*): Feverfew blooms from flower stems that rise out of nearly evergreen basal leaves. When the individual flowers begin to brown in late June, we cut off the flower stems at the base. By mid- to late August, new but shorter flower stems provide another flush of bloom. Therein lies one good reason to deadhead this plant. The other is to avoid the multitude of seeds that drop on your garden and germinate.

4. Figure SU-35. **Astilbe:** If you part the foliage of any astilbe, you will find that the flower is held above the foliage by a dedicated stem. Once an astilbe has bloomed, you can cut the flower stem at its base or leave it. More often than not, we choose to leave the dried flower, because it looks good in the garden, especially when many of a single variety are massed.

PLANTS THAT NEED TO BE GROWN IN A CONFINED SPACE: A BRIEF STORY

The late Tom Savery had a garden that swept down to the banks of the Avon River in England. Shortly after Tom bought the place in the 1980s, he discovered a 20-foot-diameter concrete ring, which turned out to be the foundation of an abandoned silo. It was set about 2 feet into the ground, its top flush with the surrounding grade. Tom dug up all the weeds and grass within the ring, dumped in topsoil, and jokingly named it his Prison Garden. He planted every invasive perennial he wanted to grow within the confines of this concrete ring and, as he said, "let them duke it out." Here are some of the herbaceous perennials we would put in our Prison Garden if we had one: mints, plume poppy (*Macleaya cordata*), gooseneck loosetrife (*Lysimachia clethroides*), butterbur (*Petasites japonicus*), some grasses such as ribbon grass (*Phalaris arundinacea* 'Picta') and giant miscanthus (*Miscanthus floridulus*), obedient plant (*Physostegia virginiana*).

5. Figures SU-36 and SU-37. **Hosta 'Sum and Substance':** As with all hostas, this chartreuse variegated hosta sends up flowers on specific flowering stems. In this pair of before-and-after shots, you can see how the removal of the unsightly spent blooms (and the one brown leaf from a nearby tree) improves the look of the plant.

6. Figure SU-38. **Candelabra primula** (*Primula japonica*): Mary is making a

choice between primulas that bloom faded pink and others that bloom burgundy red, a far more pleasing garden plant. She cuts to their base the pink flowers, and ties yellow flagging to those that bear the burgundy blooms to remind us to let those stems go to seed. Once the seedpods have ripened, we'll scatter the burgundy flower seeds in loosened soil in the same area. We'll get 100 percent germination from this reliable seed-producing perennial.

FIGURE SU-39

FIGURE SU-40

7. Figure SU-39. **Siberian iris** (*Iris sibirica*): This iris also sends up flowers on dedicated flower stems; after blooming, they are best cut off at the base.

8. Figure SU-40. **Gas plant** (*Dictamnus albus*): This plant throws its flower stem partway up a leaf stem. Mary cuts back the flower stem to the point where it intersects the leaf stem.

Like Mary, you might find it more comfortable to carry your kneeling pad with you as you deadhead (Figure SU-41), then use it to keep your knees from getting bruised. And as you can see from Figure SU-42, deadheading can produce a pretty good-looking wheelbarrow load even though it is destined for the compost pile. This photo of the wheelbarrow reminds me of a little garden maintance story.

Years ago we were at Vasterival, the garden of Princess Greta Sturdza on the Normandy coast of France, with our friend Quita Vitzthum. Princess Sturdza maintains eleven acres of exquisite woodland and sunny gardens held together

by sweeping and curving lawn paths. Many Dutch horticultural students help maintain her garden. On the day we were there, students were deadheading roses and the feverfew that she had interplanted with them. As the students worked they threw spent blooms onto large tarpaulins and into wheelbarrows near where they were working. Now, our timing for deadheading is slightly different from that of Princess Sturdza. We might not deadhead spent blooms for a few days. Not so in Normandy.

As we rounded a corner at Vasterival, I was greeted with one of the most striking garden sights to ever meet my eyes: whole tarps and whole wheelbarrows holding nothing but ever so slightly imperfect blooms of pink, red, and white roses and feverfew. And nearby, of course, perfectly maintained banks of pink, red, and white roses through which perfect white feverfew bloomed.

Figure SU-41. One of Mary's constant weeding companions is a foam-filled kneeling pad.

Figure SU-42. Even a wheelbarrow full of garden clippings can be a thing of beauty.

Figure SU-43. (Opposite) Mary's other weeding companion is a pair of pruning shears, which she keeps sharp with a diamond dust file.

Removing Invasive Plants

■

Google "invasive plants" on the Internet, and enter your state in the search box to find many sources of information on plants considered invasive (and not to be planted) in your region. People who care about the environment are realizing that nurseries and garden centers unwittingly sell invasive plants that we gardeners are buying and planting. Through seed dispersal or any number of methods, many invasives are escaping into the wild to create a serious imbalance in nature, one we may never be able to put right unless we all act responsibly. In the Northeast, for example, one result of invasives appears every October: thousands of acres of woodland awash in the bright red foliage of burning bush (*Euonymus alatus* 'Compactus'). Seedlings from residential planting have invaded surrounding woodland. Honeysuckle, Japanese knotweed, and buckthorn are also invasives. In the South it's the kudzu vine. Keep this issue of invasives in mind when you choose plants for your garden. It was the reason we removed several mature purple-leaved barberries (*Berberis thunbergii* 'Atropurpurea') and replaced them with purple-leaved ninebark (*Physocarpus opulifolius* 'Diabolo').

The problems associated with invasive plants

Figure SU-44. (Opposite) Stepping out of the garden shed, I spotted the offending party: an invasive hay-scented fern within our favorite brunnera—'Jack Frost'.

Figure SU-45. That day we wanted to remove all the hay-scented ferns we could find in the garden. As lovely as this combination looked, we know that the ferns would gradually overwhelm the brunnera.

Figure SU-46. Off with the ferns' head and roots.

are not limited to the indigenous landscape around your garden, but also right in it, as with herbaceous perennials that expand their numbers through seeds or an aggressive root system. In the Brick Walk Garden (see page 112), we removed large numbers of excessively self-seeding perennials: lady's mantle (*Alchemilla mollis*), violets, *Lobelia cardinalis*, *L. siphilitica*, and certain pulmonarias. If you don't periodically scour the entire garden for these plants, they'll quietly extend their numbers far beyond what is right for the balance of your garden.

SCOURING OUT THE HAY-SCENTED FERN

The hay-scented fern (*Dennstaedtia punctilobula*), a lovely light green fern that covers banks and woodland edges across New England, crops up in the most unexpected places. Mary and I scoured our entire garden one day looking just for hay-scented ferns to determine which we would leave and which we would uproot. Looking for one species at a time is a good way to approach the problem of invasive plants, because your eyes become attuned to their shape and color.

I was coming out of our garden shed that day carrying a shovel just as photographer Richard Brown arrived (Figure SU-44). I looked down and there among the handsome 'Jack Frost' brunnera (*Brunnera macrophylla* 'Jack Frost') I spotted a hay-scented fern. Richard saw me looking askance at what he regarded as a lovely plant

combination (see Figure SU-45). I had to admit I agreed, but only to a point. Had I left that fern in place, it would gradually have overwhelmed the brunnera.

Richard's and my different views on this one fern in that one place bring up an important point about maintenance and garden style. You, like Richard, may prefer the combination of fern and brunnera and would have left the fern where it was, knowing you could always remove it in a year or two when it had begun to kill off the brunnera. I, on the other hand, felt that the fern presented a long-term problem I wanted to resolve in the very short term; up came its roots (see Figure SU-46) and onto the burn pile it went. Had I put it on the compost pile, its teeny black elastic roots would have taken hold in the richest soil on the place. This story illustrates what Henry David Thoreau meant when he said, "Weeding is making invidious distinctions with a hoe."

That was only the beginning of the search for

Figure SU-47. (Opposite) Hay-scented ferns and freely seeding columbine had also insinuated themselves into a group of Japanese painted ferns.

Figure SU-48. Mary set to work with her hand weeder.

Figure SU-49. Mary removed the invasive ferns and other weeds to bring this small area of our garden back into focus: gray-leaved ferns next to gray lichen on granite.

PLACING A BULB ORDER

Late each summer we place a bulb order. We plant tulips only in pots because of vole problems in our beds, so we order in small quantities but a wide variety of types and colors. Here's our tulip order for fall 2005; we ordered ten of each. No bulb catalog we know compares to Brent and Becky Heath's for quality, breadth of choice, and sound cultural information: www.brentandbeckysbulbs.com.

Early: 'Monsella' (yellow-red)

Early   'Carmine Parrot' (pink-red)
to Mid: 'Daydream' (soft yellow-orange with peach-apricot)

Mid: 'Garant' (yellow)
        'Gudoshnik' (yellow-red)
        'Design Impression' (pinky red)
        'Silver Stream' (creamy yellow)
        'Princess Irene' (bright orange-purple)

Late: 'Golden Angel' (golden)
        'Black Parrot' (almost black)
        'Blushing Lady' (buff orange-yellow)
        'Cum Laude' (dark violet white and blue base)
        'Professor Rontgen' (orange)

Figure SU-50. (Opposite) After removing invasive plants, some of which might have formed fairly large colonies, we follow up with mulch. Here I'm covering recently weeded soil with 2 inches of leaf mold to rebuild the soil and prevent weeds from taking hold in the recently opened soil. Nature abhors a vacuum.

Techniques to Reduce Maintenance

Do everything right the first time. Don't take shortcuts. Do your homework.

Soil

- The base for your entire garden is the soil. Keep up the health of the soil by top-dressing with leaf mold, homemade compost, or decomposed manure as often as is practical. Fertile soil rich in organic matter ensures ease in working the soil and fewer cultural problems.
- If you're buying topsoil, check the source carefully to be certain you won't be bringing weed seeds and diseases into your garden.
- Test the soil to get a fuller understanding of what amendments you might add so your soil supports healthier plants.

Weeds and Weeding

- Weed for half an hour or so every day or two rather than for three to four hours every two weeks.
- Don't let weeds go to seed and drop their next generation on your garden. One weed can produce thousands more through its seed.
- If you have let the weeding get ahead of you, start in the area where weeds have already begun to set seed. It's the seed setting and dropping of those seeds on your garden soil that you want to prevent more than anything.
- Because weed seeds settle into the gaps between paving stones, use the largest stones you can afford, thereby reducing the amount of grouting necessary between them.
- If you have a limited time to weed before guests arrive, pay attention to where weeds are most noticeable, such as at the edges of beds. If you keep on top of the weeding, you'll be more apt to keep your garden fairly weed free.
- Mow your lawn at a height between 3 and 4 inches, and you'll see less crabgrass seed germination.
- Weed right up to the crown of plants; lift their leaves to be sure you get every last weed.
- You'll have to accept that the first year you plant a garden is the year when the most weeding will be necessary. It takes time for plants to grow and their foliage to meet and sufficiently shade the ground to slow down seed germination.

Paving Materials

- Use materials wisely in the garden: pave areas with stone tightly laid one to the next—as opposed to leaving big gaps between them—to reduce maintenance.
- Don't put brick walkways in high-

humidity, shady places; moss and algae will grow on the bricks and cause the walkway to become slippery.

- Take up poorly growing lawn paths to a depth of 4 inches or so, then put down 3 inches of crushed stone or gravel. Cover with ground cloth and then 1 inch of $^3/_8$-inch pea stone or a similar top-dressing.
- Edge a perennial garden with stone, pea stone, or gravel.
- Use mulches to keep weeds down and moisture in.

Plant Choice

- Know the cultural requirements of your plants; provide them with what they need.
- Choose plants that are right for your zone, the growing conditions in your garden, and the sun and wind exposure in the spot where you plan to plant them.
- Group plants that share common cultural requirements. Naming the gardens will help: the Dry Shade Garden, the Moisture-Tolerant Garden.
- Don't rely on watering and irrigation; plant trees, shrubs, and perennials that are right for the amount of moisture you can expect in a normal growing season.
- Design low-maintenance plantings for pots; rely on foliage or repeat bloomers for long-lasting color. Avoid plants that require deadheading.
- Choose plants that are relatively problem free.
- If you have a problem with Japanese beetles, don't plant *Corylus* (filberts) or other plants such as grapevines, which attract them.
- Know when to let plants go to seed and when to deadhead before they go to seed. Some freely seeding plants, such as *Lobelia siphilitica*, can be a pest, yet seedlings of a dark red *Primula japonica* are a treasure.
- If plants that have been in the ground for years are not performing well and perhaps are even spreading disease (such as powdery mildew in old plantings of phlox), dig up the plants and put them on the burn pile, not the compost pile.
- If shrubs are suffering because of shade from overhanging trees, transplant them.
- For less maintenance, plant shrubs, trees, and ground covers instead of perennials.
- Choose crab apples and other woody plants in part for their disease resistance so the plants look good without chemical sprays. For example, *Malus* 'Royalty' is not resistant to scab, and the disease takes most of its leaves by mid-August; the foliage on disease-resistant *Malus* 'Prairiefire', Sugar Tyme, and 'Adams', however, remains largely spotless and intact.

FIGURE SU-51

FIGURE SU-52

FIGURE SU-53

1. Figure SU-51. We lay tarps along the outer edge of a hedge, tucking one edge of each tarp under the hedge so all trimmings fall onto the tarps. This makes cleanup efficient by precluding time-consuming raking. With ear protection in place, I start at the bottom of the hedge and sweep the hedge trimmer upward, holding the blade of the trimmer parallel with and tightly into the growth. I cut as deeply as the hedge trimmer will go without scalping the hedge. I don't angle the blade into the hedge; doing so would result in gouges.

2. Figure SU-52. I hold the blade absolutely flat to the hedge. By sweeping upward, the trimmer stands far less chance of getting caught in branch tips. If the hedge trimmer does catch on a branch too large for it, I use pruning shears to cut off the branch at the appropriate depth. After rough-trimming the entire side of a hedge, I go back and clean up any stragglers by adding a downward motion and a side-to-side sweep.

3. Figure SU-53. I trim the top of the hedge, moving from the back of the hedge toward the front so that all trimmings fall onto the tarp.

4. Figure SU-54. If the hedge, or in this case the English hedge maple (*Acer campestre*), is tall enough to require a ladder, I ask that someone stand on the bottom step to steady it. (Robin is in there, behind the variegated dogwood.)

5. Figure SU-55. (Opposite) When pruning the black haw hedge (*Viburnum prunifolium*), we set three tarps along one side of the hedge to catch the trim-

FIGURE SU-54

FIGURE SU-55

FIGURE SU-56

this invasive plant. Mary discovered that hay-scented fern had insinuated itself into a group of Japanese painted ferns (*Athyrium nipponicum* 'Pictum') in the shady Rock Garden (see Figure SU-47). With her hand weeder, she carefully removed the hay-scented fern and a few other weeds (see Figure SU-48) so that, when she was finished, the offending party was in the black bucket and the painted fern could grow unimpeded (see Figure SU-49). Having removed invasive plants, we backfill the resulting hole with compost.

Hedge Trimming

A trimmed hedge imparts a sense of order to the overall garden. Crisp geometric shapes of shorn hedges offer a contrasting backdrop for the natural forms of trees, shrubs, and perennials. To maintain the yew, boxwood, and black haw (*Viburnum prunifolium*) hedges we planted over the years, I always ask for help from Pat, Robin, or Siena: they spread tarps and set up ladders adjacent to the next hedge while I'm working on the previous one. When I finish a hedge, they gather up the trimmings and take them to the compost pile. It's safe having help nearby; hedge trimming can involve balancing on a high teetery ladder with sharp power tools.

mings. Upon finishing one side and the top, we gather all the corners of two tarps and empty the trimmings onto the middle tarp, then haul it to the compost pile. After the tarps are free of trimmings, we set them along the back side of the hedge and I trim that side.

6. Figure SU-56. Several small boxwoods mark entries or path junctions throughout the garden. I shear the boxwoods with the hedge trimmer rather than hedge shears. The longer blade ensures a more uniform cut.

BEE STING REMEDY

When I was trimming the yew hedge I disturbed a nest of yellow jacket wasps. Two of them stung me before I could get out of their way. Pat immediately picked a couple of leaves from a plantain weed growing in the lawn. She told me to chew them into a pulp, then put the pulp on the spots where the wasp had stung me. The sting went away within seconds. This is no old wives' tale; it works. (See Figures SU-57 to SU-59 below.)

We always follow the same procedure:

To trim a hedge, I first gather tools and supplies.

- Several 10- by 10-foot tarps
- 6-foot and 10-foot stepladders
- Electric hedge trimmer with a sharp 24-inch-long blade. (Dull blades make the work harder.)
- Extension cords
- Pruning shears
- Hedge trimming shears
- Lawn rake
- Ear protectors
- Work gloves

Sometimes, plants at the back of a perennial bed come right up to a hedge. I don't want to spread tarps, no matter how light, over the perennials, so I trim the hedge and simply let the clippings fall to the ground. Then we rake up the clippings.

I usually trim the hedges in mid-June (after the initial spring spurt of growth) and again in mid- to late August. Any later and it would encourage shrubs to send out new growth that would be susceptible to fall frosts. If you trim a hedge in mid-July, for example, and the plant has time to put on considerable new growth, it will not have time to harden off and will be damaged especially at the tips by early autumn frosts. The timing for hedge trimming in your area may well be different, but the principles behind the timing remain similar.

COMPOSTING

Our one-and-a-half acres of garden produce a lot of compostable material, and we save every bit of it. When we weed and deadhead, when we rake up excess lawn clippings, when anything compostable comes out of the garden, we turn it into compost. And we use a pretty simple method. We pile it across the road from the garden in 5- to 7-foot-high heaps, then every week or so I shovel previously made compost, with all its microbes, onto the top of the pile. If we have a backhoe in the garden, I always ask the operator to turn the piles, but otherwise we simply let the material rot down. Once the compost is made, we cover it with black plastic or hay.

CHECKLISTS

JUNE INTO JULY

- Plant annuals in pots in late May to early June.
- Weed under and around shrubs and perennials.
- Check on the moisture level of all plants planted in spring; water if necessary.
- Deadhead *Primula japonica*, *Iris sibirica*, sweet cicely, bearded iris, ajuga, *Leucanthemum × superbum* 'Becky', and others that need it.
- Leave seed heads on peonies, baptisia,

and others that have attractive seedpods or seed heads.

- In early June, cut off the top foot of asters to keep them from getting too leggy.
- Thin out one-third of the stems in *Phlox paniculata.*
- Stake and tie tall perennials such as *Crambe cordifolia*, delphinium, and tall campanulas.
- Mow lawns weekly; mow meadow paths every other week.
- String-trim edges every two to three weeks; string-trim woodlands twice a year to keep shoots from coming up where trees or saplings have been removed.
- Remove invasive and aggressive plants such as lobelia, feverfew, and tradescantia.
- After bearded iris bloom, take them up and divide; do this every three to five years.
- Now that the foliage is fully out, cut out any deadwood in trees and shrubs.
- Fertilize annuals in pots weekly throughout the summer; water pots every three days or when needed, depending on rainfall.
- After July 4, cut back daffodil foliage in lawns and where it shows in garden beds.
- Remove spent blooms from daylilies daily.
- Place bulb orders, including paperwhites for forcing.
- Prune or shear back new growth on any plants that you're training.

JULY INTO AUGUST

- Cut back foliage of hardy geraniums, but leave new central green leaves.
- Assess lower tree branches to see if any of them should be removed to bring more sunlight into gardens under them.
- Weed weekly; don't get behind.
- Deadhead, and remove spent blooms from daylilies daily.
- Now that *Phlox divaricata* has gone to seed in the woodland, string-trim it to scatter seed, to create a denser planting.
- Trim hedges.
- Feed potted plants weekly and water them every three days or so as needed.
- In this hot, dry time of year, give sufficient water to all drought-susceptible plants, such as *Fothergilla gardenii*, astilbe, and especially plants in dry, hot areas of the garden.
- Summer-prune water sprouts on crab apple and standard apple trees; also prune off sprouts shooting up from the base of the trunks of crab apple trees.
- Assess new growth on plants you are training to see if pruning is required.

Laying Stone or Brick Edging

Long, linear edges or broad, sinuous curves can accommodate stone or brick paving, real time-savers when it comes to edge maintenance. Stone or brick can be laid horizontally to form a 12- to 18-inch-wide paved edge, onto which floppy perennials such as hardy geraniums or catmint can spread. Stone or brick laid in a 24-inch-wide edge doubles as a path. Or you can lay stones vertically along a bed edge. A series of tightly abutting 12-inch-wide pieces of cut stone on edge (with 10 inches below ground and 2 inches above) will keep lawn grasses on one side and perennials on the other.

Establish vertical edges by burying all but 2 inches of the brick, cut stone, or fieldstone on edge or on end in tamped crushed gravel. Avoid plastic edging or green painted aluminum; neither has much substance or aesthetic appeal, and they don't stay put.

Edging material and the way it is set should reflect the tone and mood of the garden. Look throughout your existing garden and the exterior of your home to see what, if any, stone or brick already exists, and repeat these materials for coherence. Too many materials look busy.

Keep in mind that you affect the mood created by each paving material by the way you lay it. Mortar new bricks tightly and you create one feeling; set old bricks in sandy loam and let moss grow between them and you create a completely different mood.

Cut Stone

Geometric cut stone laid horizontally looks most appropriate to edge straight beds. Cut stone laid vertically can edge straight or curvilinear beds. Set a series of 18-inch-wide by 36-inch-long cut stones horizontally, tight and end to end, and you simultaneously create edging and a path (see Figure LS-1). Set 12- to 18-inch-wide cut stones of random lengths vertically end to end with only 1 to 2 inches showing above grade and you'll make a less dramatic, less formal statement, although the edge will function to keep lawn and clover

Figure LS-1. Edging a perennial bed with 12- to 18-inch-wide stone set horizontally allows plants at the edge of the beds to flop onto stone rather than lawn. The depth of the base under these horizontally laid stones can be less than shown in this illustration if your soil is freely draining.

from creeping into your beds (see Figure LS-2). Cut stone, typically limestone, sandstone, or marble, sells for about six dollars per square foot. All can be set vertically or horizontally.

Fieldstone

Fieldstone, which is randomly shaped, is most appropriate for curving and straight gardens or around relaxed herb or vegetable gardens. Fieldstone looks most settled when it is indigenous. The material's informality comes from its rough surfaces and from its irregular shape, which leaves random gaps between stones laid flat and an irregular line along the top of vertically set edging stones. Gaps between horizontally set fieldstones can be infilled with sandy loam to support thyme or moss; mortared gaps look less charming but will better fend off clover and grasses. Fieldstone costs two to three dollars per square foot or you may find an abundance of them on your property. (See Figures LS-1 and LS-2 for directions on how to lay fieldstone vertically and horizontally.)

Brick

Edging with brick is especially appropriate when your home, or even just its chimney, is brick. Old paving bricks are best, because they lend a settled feeling of age to a perennial or mixed border or an herb garden. Old brick is not always available, though, and can be twice as costly as new brick. The manufactured look of new brick can be toned down by planting thyme or other ground-hugging perennials, such as arabis, nearby so it will creep over horizontally set edging bricks. (See Figure LS-3 for directions on how to lay brick horizontally.) You can also set bricks on end vertically, with only 2 inches showing above ground (see Figure LS-4), to form a simple terra-cotta line down the length of a straight or curving bed. Avoid setting bricks on end at

Figure LS-2. The same 12- to 18-inch-wide stone can be set vertically with 1 to 2 inches showing above grade to form a clean, crisp edging line along the front of a perennial border. The edging will keep the lawn out of the bed, although you'll still have to run a string trimmer along the edge to keep the lawn grass low.

an angle. The resulting jagged series of little peaks along the length of the edges looks busy and unattractive. Bricks cost between forty cents and a dollar each, depending on age and quality. Purchase only hard pavers (often called clinker brick), which, when knocked together, clink instead of clunk. Bricks with a soft interior—clunkers—eventually disintegrate.

Basic Foundation for Most Edging Materials

When laying brick or stone vertically, excavate 2 to 4 inches below where the bottom edge of the material will lie. For example, if you will bury at least 6 inches of an 8-inch brick, excavate down 8 to 10 inches below the existing grade. Backfill with 2 to 4 inches of finely crushed gravel or crusher dust—a fine by-product of the stone crushing process. Wet it with a hose, then tamp it soundly with a tamper. Set the bricks on end, then backfill to within 2 to 3 inches of the finish grade with the same crushed gravel; tamp, then backfill the top 2 to 3 inches with topsoil.

To determine the depth of excavation for horizontal stone or brick edging, add 6 inches to the thickness of the edging material itself. For example, to establish a sound base for 3-inch-thick bricks, excavate down 9 inches, then backfill with 6 inches of crushed gravel or sand. Wet the base material, tamp, then lay the bricks. Use the same base material to fill between them.

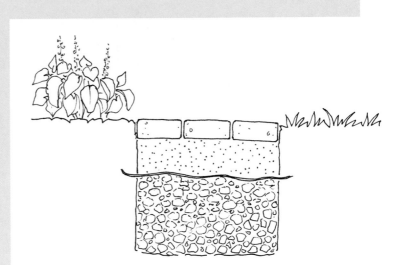

Figure LS-3. Brick, like cut stone, laid horizontally provides a low-maintenance edge for a perennial garden. Edging plants can flop onto the brick, and one wheel of a lawn mower can run atop the outermost brick to keep lawn grass at the appropriate height without having to string-trim the edge.

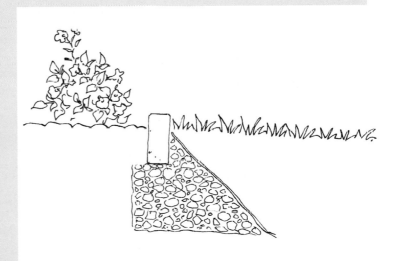

Figure LS-4. Brick can also be laid on edge or on end. This approach means you lay only one brick vertically as opposed to three horizontally, as in Figure LS-3. However, you'll have to trim the lawn along the vertical edge every week or two to keep it at an appropriate height.

Autumn

Figure AU-1. (Opposite) Part of the reason why the fall garden looks so good is that five of the six primary and secondary colors are visible at once: red, orange, and yellow leaves, green lawn, blue sky. Only violet is missing to come round the color wheel. **Figure AU-2.** The meadow, and the path I mow weekly through it to three pin oaks, provides a backdrop for all views east from our garden. Philip Ranney, son of the farmer next door, mows the meadow three times every season, and feeds the thousand bales of hay he gathers from it to his herd of eighty Jersey cows every winter.

THINKING ABOUT THE GARDEN IN WINTER is analogous to planning a family trip; spring is about getting to the destination and sharing those wonderful moments of arrival. Summer is about all the experiences your family enjoys while there, and fall is coming home. Gardening, and dare I say the family trip as well, is not just about enjoying the summer; it's about enjoying and engaging everyone in the other three stages as well.

This analogy gets right to the heart of gardening. Maintenance and all the work it involves renews us, yet sometimes wears us out. Of course it's work; of course it demands exertion and effort and time. But if you carry out every act of garden maintenance mindfully, with care and thought about the moment at hand, deep satisfaction results. As I sit in my office in the barn writing this book in the dead of winter, I look out at the results of twenty-five years of work that Mary and I have put into this garden. Dark yew hedges draw clean lines in the

Figure AU-3. Many mornings, mists come off the meadow and into our autumn garden to suffuse the whole place with a kind of mystery. The red fruits on the Donald Wyman crab apple will last until March.

snow; red and yellow fruits hang from the crab apple trees where blue jays perch; I can see the orange-red stems of the Winter Flame dogwoods we planted last spring against the arborvitae hedge. I can't tell you how rewarding that is.

Yet just eight weeks ago we were hard at it. As we worked on and off from early October to the end of November, we were surrounded by orange, red, and yellow leaves that glowed against the blue sky and green lawn. All those leaves had to be raked and composted. All those perennials that had given us so much pleasure emerging in spring, flowering in summer, and heading back into the ground in fall had to be cut back.

We raked and mowed, raked and mowed; we emptied terra-cotta pots and took them—and the outdoor furniture and gates—into the barn. We top-dressed the beds when we could find the time and energy. And as we approached the end, when nearly all the leaves were raked and the perennials cut back, we walked through the garden and could see its bare bones for the first time since last spring. The evergreens and hedges, the stone walls and garden shed, the new little bridge we put in, and the pinky red fruits on the new mountain ash (*Sorbus alnifolia*) that we planted last spring came to the foreground.

Before we even realize it, we're back inside, looking out. The green lawn gives way to white snow under a blue sky. As we look north out of the dining room windows, we can see the gray stone wall that Dan Snow built for us a few years ago with its cap of snow. Hemlocks just behind the wall provide a backdrop to the smooth gray lines of the yellowwood tree.

Cutting Back Perennials

By mid-September, our perennials are beginning to look a little ragged. By the end of September, following one or two nights when temperatures drop below freezing, it's time to start cutting back these plants. We do so for a variety of reasons: by removing the stems and foliage, we are removing insects and diseases; getting them out of the garden means we'll be able to rake leaves from the beds when the trees' leaves begin to fall; and we have to cut back perennials sometime because next year's growth needs room.

Early spring is the only other time to cut back perennials before new shoots begin to emerge, and that's not a good time for such work. To get the work done then, we would have to walk on moist, wet soil among broken plants weighed down by snow and a winter's worth of decomposed leaves, rotten stems, and general mayhem. With everything else that has to be accomplished in spring, it simply makes sense to cut back the perennials in autumn. During the first half of September and most of October, we go through the garden in three stages.

FIGURE AU-4

FIGURE AU-5

Figure AU-4. Ligularia and many other late-flowering perennials bloom from late August into September; by mid-September the flowers have browned and shriveled.

Figure AU-5. Even though we will cut these plants to the ground within the month, I still cut back the spent flower stems, and any leaves with a lot of holes in them. I part the leaves and run my pruning shears down the full length of the flower and leaf stems, then snip them off as close to the ground as I can get.

FIGURE AU-6

Figure AU-6. The result is a clean, handsome perennial that will hold this look, depending on the number of hard frosts, for another two to three weeks.

MID- TO LATE SEPTEMBER

We follow cues provided by the idiosyncracies of certain plants. We start by cutting back:

1. Plants with foliage that yellows or ripens early. Bloodroot (*Sanguinaria canadensis*) and bleeding heart (*Dicentra* (now *Lamprocapnos*) *spectabilis*) are two examples.

2. Diseased plants such as peonies that are sometimes shriveled from the effects of botrytis, or *Phlox paniculata*, bee balm, and helianthus that have gray patches of powdery mildew on their leaves, or holly-

FIGURE AU-7

FIGURE AU-8

FIGURE AU-9

Figure AU-7. This is a peony/hardy geranium bed before I cut it back.

Figure AU-8. I cut back most of the perennials in this bed but left many of the hardy geraniums with long-lasting foliage as well as hostas and maidenhair ferns for cutting back later in the month.

Figure AU-9. Once the tarp is of a weight that is still comfortable for me to drag, I draw two corners of the tarp together, twist them to form a kind of handle, and haul the tarp to the compost pile. We use the same method to haul prunings or leaves.

Figure AU-10. Pat cuts back daylilies. Because she has to be careful with her back, she puts the cut stems into a wheelbarrow and takes small loads to the compost pile rather than dragging a heavily loaded tarp.

Figure AU-11. Pat discovered a clever tool for cutting back perennials with fleshy stems, such as daylilies and hosta: an inexpensive serrated kitchen knife. She gathers all the stems in one hand, tugs on the stems to create tension, and with the other hand cuts through the stems.

hocks with brown rust spots on the foliage.

3. Hosta leaves that are badly damaged by slugs, or *Crambe cordifolia* leaves chewed by earwigs and caterpillars.

4. The leaves of certain daylilies that flop or are lying flat on the ground. (Cut back floppy or flat daylilies in early August, and they will regenerate upstanding foliage and look fresh and new by early September.)

5. The entire stems of feverfew, *Lobelia cardinalis*, and *L. siphilitica*, to avoid excessive self-seeding.

EARLY TO MID-OCTOBER

1. We cut off only the flower stalks and unsightly stems of plants that have fresh green basal leaves (which we leave in place going into winter): hollyhocks, *Leucanthemum* × *superbum* 'Becky', digitalis, and verbascum.

2. We completely cut back daylilies, catmint, helenium, echinacea, doronicum, and any other perennials that look unsightly at this time of year.

MID- TO LATE OCTOBER

We completely cut back:

1. Plants that hold a scattering of blooms into late October in a particularly warm autumn: turtlehead (*Chelone lyonii*), fall-blooming anemone (*Anemone tomentosa*

× 'Robustissima'), *Helenium* 'Riverton Beauty', *Aster* 'Purple Dome', Joe Pye weed (*Eupatorium rugosum* 'Chocolate').

2. Many late-blooming astilbes, the seed heads of which we leave on for 2 to 3 months after the bloom has gone by.

3. Plants that have stayed robust and intact well into October: pulmonaria, dictamnus, lamium, everlasting bleeding heart (*Dicentra eximia*), heuchera, euphorbia, many ferns, fragaria, many hardy geraniums, Siberian iris, lamb's ears (*Stachys byzantina*), *Kirengeshoma palmata*, ligularia, and epimedium.

4. Many hostas, *Thalictrum rochebrunianum,* and amsonia, whose leaves turn golden or yellow and add considerably to the autumn garden.

5. Variegated perennials with foliage that looks good well into October: *Brunnera macrophylla* 'Jack Frost', Solomon's seal (*Polygonatum odoratum* 'Variegatum').

WE DON'T CUT BACK:

1. Plants that add winter interest to the garden: many ornamental grasses, especially *Miscanthus* with its stiff, stout stems (as opposed to the wispier *Panicum virgatum*).

2. Perennials that benefit from not being cut back, such as some daylilies, and perennials with reliably evergreen leaves: *Waldsteinia ternata*, *Geranium macrorrhizum*, many species of pulmonaria, heuchera, European ginger (*Asarum europaeum*), Christmas fern, ajuga, and Oriental poppies, which send up new green growth every September in preparation for their blooming next early summer. If you're unsure whether or not to cut back any plants in your garden, leave them for a while and see what condition they're in by late autumn. If they're withered and brown, cut them back; if they're green and healthy, let them be.

3. Massed plants that have interesting seedpods or seed heads that look good poking up out of the snow, such as black-eyed Susan (*Rudbeckia fulgida* 'Goldsturm'), *Sedum spectabile* (now *Hylotelephium*) 'Autumn Joy'. We do not leave any of these if there is only one here and one there.

4. Russian sage (*Perovskia atriplicifolia*) and other woody subshrubs that are best left intact through the winter, then cut back in spring, when you can clearly see what wood has been killed off by winter.

5. Bearded iris, which is best left intact so rainwater drains from its downwardly arcing leaves. If you cut off the tops to make them look pretty, rainwater gathers atop the cut and seeps down into the rhizomes and can cause rot. Having said that, many people cut the spotted tops off the leaves to create a handsome fan and let the plant go into the winter that way.

CUTTING BACK A SINGLE AREA OF OUR GARDEN

FIGURE AU-12

FIGURE AU-13

Figure AU-12. Because most of the perennials in the Long Borders have woody or stiff stems, we use pruning shears. We cut stems close to ground level so the rake tines won't catch, and leaves won't be trapped in the stubs. We start cutting back the perennials, just as the trees and shrubs begin to shed their leaves.

Figure AU-13. Pat gets started cutting back the Long Borders in early October. We go the length of these beds in two or three stages. Pat is removing the unsightly foliage of daylilies and other perennials that are nipped by early frosts.

Figure AU-14. A couple of weeks later, Siena cuts back purple-leaved snakeroot (*Cimicifuga ramosa* (now *Actaea simplex*) 'Brunette'), one of our favorite fall-blooming perennials, but for winter interest she leaves the dramatic beige foliage of purple reed grass (*Miscanthus sinensis* 'Purpurascens') as well as the still-intact foliage of Joe Pye weed (*Eupatorium maculatum* 'Gateway').

Figure AU-15. (Opposite) Because we don't see the Long Borders during the winter from the house, and because snow impedes winter walks, we cut back most ornamental grasses, but we do save a lot of their beautiful stems for arrangements.

FIGURE AU-14

Figure AU-16. This year we placed the cut ornamental grass stems in 3-foot-high urns, and displayed them under the cover of the barn. Because we enter the house through the barn, these huge arrangements, which remain intact for months, give us a lot of pleasure throughout the winter.

Figure AU-17. As we cut back perennials, we throw them onto a tarp for easy hauling. This time of year, the compost pile grows exponentially.

Figure AU-18. Four of us cut back this garden in about three hours, although Pat and the others had been cutting back smaller perennials on and off for the month preceding this big day of work.

Figure AU-19. To speed up the process in the Woodland Garden, we cut back low, wispy perennials such as foamflower (*Tiarella cordifolia*), woodland phlox (*Phlox divaricata*), and *Phlox stolonifera* with a string trimmer, then rake up the results.

Figure AU-20. Here's what the Woodland Garden looks like once I've finished string trimming. We leave the foliage of ornamental grasses for the entire winter if we can see the plants from the house.

Figure AU-21. Certain plants such as these hostas look so good in late fall that we don't cut them back until their leaves turn to mush.

Figure AU-22. We leave the foliage of ornamental grasses for the entire winter if we can see the plants from the house.

Figure AU-23. The tips and edges of bearded iris leaves can look ragged and spotted by early September. Some people let such leaves go into winter uncut so rainwater does not travel down the interior of the stem to rot out the rhizome. Rather it falls onto an intact leaf and drains off.

Figure AU-24. If you're a tidy gardener like Pat, she cuts back the fans of bearded iris foliage to where they look sound. After several killing frosts, these leaves will have yellowed and flopped over. We cut that largely decomposed foliage back in spring.

TECHNIQUES FOR CUTTING BACK PERENNIALS

- To cut back perennials that have many thin stems growing from a central crown, such as catmint, sweep one hand to gather all the stems, thereby exposing their base. With pruning shears, cut the stems as close to the ground as possible.
- To cut back fleshier stemmed perennials that form a many-leaved crown, such as daylilies,

hosta, and Siberian iris, sweep your hand in a circular motion to gather the leaves and expose their base on one side of the plant. With an old long serrated kitchen knife or a pruning saw, cut off the leaves at their base. This works well as long as you maintain pressure on the leaves against which the knife or saw can work.

- To cut back stiffer stemmed perennials such as aster, astilbe, helenium, helianthus, or phlox, which do not have evergreen basal leaves, grab a handful of stems and bend them back to create tension in the stems. With pruning shears, cut them at the base.

- To cut back stiffer-stemmed plants that have evergreen basal leaves, such as *Leucanthemum* × *superbum* 'Becky', hollyhock, or verbascum, cut each stem individually by sliding your pruning shears down the stem until you get to the base. Avoid cutting the green basal leaves.

- For low plants with wispy stems such as woodland phlox, epimedium, and maidenhair ferns, which can blanket a woodland garden, use a string trimmer, then rake up the cuttings. It's noisy but it speeds up the process.

TO COMPOST OR NOT TO COMPOST

We throw the vast proportion of stems and foliage that result from cutting back right onto the compost pile. However, if leaves or stems of perennials show any signs of disease such as powdery mildew, the wilting effects of botrytis, or rust on hollyhocks, we put those stems on the burn pile. If we have cut back perennials such as feverfew that have huge numbers of ripened seeds, we also put them on the burn pile. The seeds will last for ages in a compost pile and would germinate when we threw the resulting compost onto our beds.

Dividing Plants

DIVIDING AND TRANSPLANTING

Here's a brief story about dividing plants and how persistence can turn one plant into a multitude. Howard Andros was my mentor in the early 1980s. One spring, when we were admiring the remarkable display of double bloodroot in his garden, he told me this story. Around 1955 a friend of Howard's discovered a patch of bloodroot (*Sanguinaria canadensis*) blooming in his woodland outside Dayton, Ohio. The blooms did not have the normal eight petals but sixty-four. The following mid-September, the time to divide bloodroot, Howard's friend dug up five rhizomes and sent four to botanical gardens across the country and one to Howard.

Howard planted it, and the following fall he dug and divided it, and then he had two. The next year he did the same and had four, the next year eight, the next year sixteen, and so on. When I met Howard in the early 1980s, he had well over 100,000 divisions and had become one of the country's primary suppliers to mail-order nurseries of *Sanguinaria canadensis* 'Flore Pleno'. Howard gave us eight divisions many years ago, and we now have at least two hundred.

DIVIDING DAYLILIES

You can divide virtually any herbaceous plant that has a crown (rather than a taproot), though you may not want to end up with 100,000 divisions. Daylilies, for example, one of the most popular and dependable perennials for most American gardens, are also one of the most readily divided. Taking a division of a four- to five-year-old plant can be as simple as driving a straight-nosed spade (or a stout spading fork) down through the middle of a daylily crown (see Figure AU-25) in spring before the foliage gets too high, or in fall after you've cut back the foliage. Then simply force the handle of your spade down toward the ground and a division of the kind you see in Figure AU-26) will pop up. A division of this size could in turn be divided into six to eight small divisions if you are willing to take your time and work carefully with spading forks rather than shovels, so you keep the roots intact.

The classic method you can use to divide big, clumpy divisions of any plant such as this daylily or the ornamental grasses in the next section, is shown in Figure AU-27. Drive two spading forks into a large division of an herbaceous perennial with the backs of the forks close to and facing each other. Then push the two handles away from each other, and you'll pull the roots apart, creating two plants where you had one.

DIVIDING ORNAMENTAL GRASSES

Use this same techniques to divide ornamental grasses, though because of their dense, intertwined root systems, grasses are more difficult to divide.

Figure AU-25. Pat has already taken a large division from this daylily with a straight-nosed spade. She could have used a spading fork instead.

Figure AU-26. This is the division Pat took from a ten-year-old daylily. She can break it into five or six divisions using two spading forks and a method illustrated in Figure AU-27.

Perennial   E. Frau

Figure AU-27. Use one spading fork to uproot the crown of a perennial; use two forks back-to-back to pry apart the crown into smaller divisions.

Figure AU-28. Siena cut around half the perimeter of this eight-year-old ornamental grass root system to loosen its edge from the sorrounding soil. She then drove a spading fork into the center of the crown to pry free this large division.

Figure AU-29. Here is a close-up of the section of the main crown she has loosened.

Figure AU-30. Using two spading forks back-to-back, Siena will separate the entangled roots to create three or four divisions.

Look closely at Figure AU-28 and you'll see that Siena has first gone around half of the perimeter of a variegated miscanthus (*Miscanthus sinenesis* 'Variegatus') with a shovel to sever some of the outer roots from the main divisions she intends to take. Being heavier and stronger, I would have left the outer roots intact, but Siena needed a head start so she could manage the dividing.

She then went into the interior of the plant and drove her spading fork down into its crown (see Figure AU-28), then forced the handle of her fork down toward one ground to release the division (see Figure AU-29). A division this size could in turn be divided into two or three others using the method shown in Figure AU-27.

Dan Snow's Advice on the Body and Other Tools

My body is my most important tool. I need to keep aware of it throughout the day, especially near the end of my work time when I'm getting tired. If I'm working with another person, my main job for the day is to keep the other person safe. I focus on what the stone is doing in the light of where the other person's hands and feet are. Accidents happen fast. Be vigilant and be ready to move quickly.

Don't ask the body to go beyond its limits. It's never worth it for a stone. I ask myself all the time, "What do I have to do today to be able to come back to work tomorrow?" A stretching routine done before starting work is the best insurance against having sore muscles at the end of the day.

It is especially important not to twist when lifting a stone. If I have to lift a stone, then move to the right or left with it, I first lift the stone onto my upper thighs in a semisquat, then I pivot on the balls of my feet to face the direction I'm going rather than twisting my body. There is an old French saying that I often recall when I'm not paying attention and make a mistake in lifting: "Pain is the craft entering into the apprentice."

Wear gloves that fit well, but don't expect gloves to help you grip wet stones.

Safety glasses deflect flying stone chips and reduce the amount of dust that blows into your eyes over the course of a day.

Having too many tools on the job site can be a disadvantage. They get underfoot, get lost, and distract me from the stone. By having a few carefully chosen tools at hand and using them creatively, I keep the job simple.

I generally take with me two sizes of pry bars: a 3-foot pinch bar, and a 16-inch pry bar that looks like a large screwdriver. It's important to make lots of small pries rather than one large movement that forces the body into vulnerable positions. There is no need to make grand gestures when you need only to use a lot of 1-inch lifts with a pinch bar and a properly placed fulcrum. This is especially true when moving a stone along the ground; slide the stone just a few inches at a time.

The other tools I always have with me are two different size mash hammers (which look like wood-splitting mauls), each with a squared end and a wedge-shaped end. The 3-pound mash hammer is good for trimming and breaking up or splitting stones in the 10- to 50-pound range. For stones heavier than 50 pounds, I use an 8-pound mash hammer.

DIVIDING CATMINT AND OTHER SMALLER PERENNIALS

Dividing catmint (*Nepeta × faassenii* 'Walker's Low') is even simpler. The sequence for this plant is the same for countless herbaceous perennials with a central crown.

1. Figure AU-31. The plant in mid-September before cutting it back.
2. Figure AU-32. Cutting back the plant.
3. Figure AU-33. Driving a straight-nosed spade (or you could use a spading fork) down through the middle of the crown, then separating the division from the intact portion.
4. Figure AU-34. Backfilling the resulting hole with compost. When the plant wakes up in spring, its roots will thrive in the rich soil.
5. Figure AU-35. To divide a hardy geranium (*Geranium macrorrhizum* 'Ingwersen's Variety'), I simply drove my shovel into its edge, lifted a division of the plant, and transplanted it elsewhere in the garden. I then backfilled the resulting hole with compost. The method is the same for taking a division of catmint, daylilies, helenium, astilbe, pulmonaria, Shasta daisy, ferns, coreopsis, campanula, sedum, physostegia, and bee balm.

FIGURE AU-31

FIGURE AU-32

Figure AU-33

Figure AU-34

Figure AU-35

FIGURE AU-36

FIGURE AU-37

FIGURE AU-38

DIVIDING PEONIES

Peonies are a different matter. One of my mentors when I first started seriously learning about plants in the late 1970s was Alice Holway. She had been the main plantsperson for Senator George Aiken when he owned the Putney Nursery in southern Vermont. Alice once told me, "The best time to transplant peonies is on September 15, around noon."

If you do it right, the way serious Chinese gardeners do it, peony divisions will supposedly bloom for a century. The serious gardener will spend half a day dividing an important peony. Here's a slightly less arduous process that works.

1. Dig a hole that's 2 feet across and 2 feet deep.
2. Backfill half the depth of the hole with composted manure or composted garden trimmings.
3. Figure AU-36. Add about five shovelfuls of wood ashes. Then mix them thoroughly into the bottom half of the hole.
4. Tamp down the soil with the soles of your shoes topsoil, so it will settle as little as possible as it breaks down over the next few years.
5. Select a peony crown that you want to divide in your garden. Cut off all stems and, with a spading fork, work your way around the perimeter loosening the plant until you can lift the entire root system out of the ground. Gently pull it apart into discrete plants. Atop the division, find the red buds that will give rise to the new flowering and foliage stems in spring (see Figure AU-37).
6. Figure AU-38. Set the division into the newly prepared hole so that the red tips of the shoots will be $1\frac{1}{2}$ to 2 inches below grade when you backfill flush with the surrounding ground. If you look closely, you'll notice that we have not yet totally backfilled.
7. Cover the red shoots to a depth of no more than $1\frac{1}{2}$ to 2 inches. Use topsoil at the surface to which no animal-based manure compost has been added (it encourages the growth of fungi and may lead to botrytis, a disease that withers the above-ground stems of peonies).
8. Cover the backfilled area with 3 inches of pine needles or straw if you're transplanting in fall. Remove the mulch in spring.

DIVIDING HERBACEOUS PERENNIALS

Every autumn or spring, one of the jobs that we simply have to do, yet we often find a reason not to, is dividing herbaceous perennials. It's hard work to divide a clump of ornamental grass. It's much easier to say it looks so good during the winter that we should just let it grow for another year. The reality is that *Miscanthus sinensis* 'Purpurascens', and many other perennials, benefit from division. Divide perennials and transplant the divisions and your garden stays young and flourishes. Don't divide and your garden gets musty and old.

Figure AU-39. The cylindrical bulb planter is an efficient tool for planting a lot of bulbs in a short period of time.

Figure AU-40. Siena drives the bulb planter into the ground to its full depth, then lifts it out. The soil stays inside the cylindrical planter, thereby leaving a hole.

Siberian iris is a good example. It spreads from the perimeter of the plant; its interior dies off. When we divide Siberian iris, we take divisions from the exterior and discard the stemless interior. We take divisions of daylilies practically whenever we want to. But the problem with taking divisions is not the when and the why, it's finding the time, the energy, and the resolve to get down to it.

Planting Bulbs

PLANTING BULBS IN THE GROUND

To avoid having to look at the browning, unsightly foliage of daffodils and other bulbs after they have bloomed, we plant bulbs next to perennials, the foliage of which comes up after the bulbs have bloomed to cover their ripening foliage. Perennials with a relaxed habit, such as catmint, daylilies, ferns, and hostas, help hide unsightly bulb foliage until we cut it down after July 4. Perennials with a more upright habit and woody stems, such as phlox, helenium, and cimicifuga, are not as effective.

We use one of two tools to plant daffodils, alliums, and other large bulbs:

Figure AU-41. Siena places the bulb, roots down, into the hole, then backfills with the original soil.

Figure AU-42. An alternative to a bulb planter is to dig a hole perhaps 12 inches deep and wide, then backfill half full with compost-enriched topsoil.

Figure AU-43. Place the bulbs about 8 inches below grade atop the enriched soil, then backfill with the soil you removed to make the hole.

BULB PLANTER An 18-inch-wide cross handle is set atop a roughly 3-foot-long handle, at the bottom of which is a tapered cylinder about 10 inches long (see Figure AU-39). If we are planting a lot of bulbs over a broad area, we use this tool. As you can see in Figure AU-40, Siena drives the cylinder into the ground, then pulls it out; because of the taper on the cylinder, the soil comes with it, thereby producing a hole. We sprinkle a bit of bulb booster in the bottom of the hole, set the bulb into it (see Figure AU-41), then backfill the hole. We do not water after planting.

SHOVEL If we are planting a smaller quantity of bulbs in areas near the house or within perennial borders, we plant bulbs in groups of five or seven by simply digging several 18-inch-diameter holes about 14 inches deep (see Figure AU-42). We backfill the holes to within 6 to 8 inches of ground level with compost, sprinkle in bulb booster, turn the mixture, and set the bulbs on it (see Figure AU-43). We then fill the hole with the topsoil we removed. Siena planted this group of daffodils behind a large-leaved ligularia, the foliage of which will cover the ripening foliage of the daffodil after it blooms.

Because smaller bulbs, such as *Allium* 'Hair' (Figure AU-44), need to be planted in a shallow hole, we dig a hole about a foot deep, backfill with a mix of compost and topsoil, lay the bulbs atop the enriched mix (Figure AU-45), and cover them to the appropriate depth (Figure AU-46). In this case I put 2 to 3 inches of compost atop the bulbs, then mulched the area with 2 inches of pine needles (which I remove in spring).

Figure AU-44. Tiny bulbs should be planted in compost-enriched holes dug with a shovel.

Figure AU-45. To plant tiny allium bulbs, I dug an 8-inch-deep hole, backfilled it with 5 inches of compost-enriched soil, then set the bulbs atop it.

Figure AU-46. I covered the bulbs with 2 to 3 inches of compost-enriched soil, then mulched with 2 inches of leaf mold. After the bulbs have bloomed, the foliage of the nearby catmint will cover the yellowing foliage of the allium.

Planting Tulips in Pots

Because mice and voles often destroy tulips planted directly in the garden, we plant tulips in pots after removing the annuals that we had planted in them in early June. I follow a sequence of jobs that you could use as a model.

1. Figure AU-47. In early October, I take the pots with the spent soilless mix still in them to the edges of beds, pour the mix into the beds, and spread it around. If I have time, I fork it in. This mix, being primarily peat moss, lightens our heavy clay soil.

2. Figure AU-48. I spread the empty pots on tarps laid out on the drive-way to ease the cleanup later.

3. Figure AU-49. Because some of the pots are large, and because I want to be certain they drain well, I place 2-quart or 1-gallon plastic containers, saved from spring planting, upside down in the bottom of the pots.

4. Figure AU-50. I fill the pots to about 6 to 8 inches shy of the rim with pure soilless mix, keeping Brent and Becky Health's bulb catalog handy to know at exactly what depth they recommend each tulip be planted. (We set most 7 to 8 inches below the rim.)

5. Figure AU-51. We order about twenty
varieties in quantities of ten to twenty.
Here are ten *Tulipa* 'Blushing Lady' (late
blooming, buff orange and yellow).

6. Figure AU-52. To create greater interest,
we combine two varieties in a single pot.

Here we combined two midseason tulips
of comparable height: *Tulipa* 'Garant'
blooms, with yellow flowers, and *Tulipa*
'Gudoshnik', with yellow and red
blooms.

7. Figure AU-53. I backfill all the pots.

8. Figure AU-54. With Robin's help I carry the planted pots into the cold part of the cellar, which stays just above freezing for the winter. I water the pots well, and do so monthly until early April, when we bring them up for the spring.

Overwintering Some Annuals

Figure AU-55. (Opposite) *Acidanthera*, a semihardy bulb in Zone 4, produces its white blooms in September. Wanting to be certain that we'll have it for the garden next year, Siena uses a fork to loosen all of the bulblets, which grow just below the surface.

Storing for Winter

Figure AU-56. Not all annuals are banished to the compost pile. We overwinter some. Here I'm transplanting several *Colocasia esculenta* 'Illustris' and *Carex buchananii* pots filled with soilless mix. I'll cut back the *Colocasia* foliage 3 inches or so above its crown, but I'll leave the *Carex* grass intact. I won't water the plants at all for the winter and will store them in the cold part of the cellar, where the temperature remains at around 36 degrees F.

Figure AU-57. We cut off the acidanthera foliage with pruning shears and store the bulbs in open-mesh bags the part of the cellar that stays around 40 to 50 degrees F for the winter.

Figure AU-58. (Opposite) As long as leaves are dry and well scattered, the mulcher on this lawn tractor will pick them up and shred them, so they will turn readily into compost.

Figure AU-59. I pile the mulched leaves across the road from the garden, and rainwater and time will turn the pile into rich, dark leaf mold.

Leaf Management

Every mid-October, the garden is carpeted with leaves from all our trees: the maples, black locusts, black cherries, and ash trees that ring the garden; the apple trees, Japanese tree lilacs, birches, stewartias, crab apples, lilacs, viburnums, hydrangeas, and the cork tree, which grow within the garden; and the hundred or so mature native trees along the hedgerow across from the garden. I can tell you that it is one major project to gather these leaves and compost them, but we've been doing it for twenty-five years. The minute that leaves start to fall, I begin gathering them up before they get wet and heavy. When they get wet, they mat down and can destroy the crowns of herbaceous perennials. So we rake and rake and rake, and we store the results east or south of the garden so the leaves don't blow back onto it again. We also pile them away from the compost, so we are sure that the leaf mold stays free of weed and perennial seeds. Over the years we have created great piles of leaf mold, ready to go back onto the gardens each spring.

Figure AU-60. Robin uses a leaf blower to get leaves out of areas where raking would be inefficient.

LEAF COLLECTION WITH A RAKE, LAWN TRACTOR, AND MULCHER ATTACHMENT

In mid-October, when the leaves start to fall here in southern Vermont, I get right to work with the rake and the lawn tractor and its mulcher attachment. We rake leaves from the beds onto the lawn path, then I use the mulcher attachment on the lawn tractor to pick up and break down the leaves in one swoop (Figure AU-58).

When the collection bags are full, I drive them to the leaf mold pile behind a woodpile that acts as a barrier so the leaves can't blow away (see Figure AU-59). Every few days during the fall, I scatter a wheelbarrow load of compost or topsoil over this pile to introduce microbes, which hasten the breakdown of mulched leaves into nutrient-rich compost.

APPROPRIATE USES FOR A GAS-POWERED LEAF BLOWER

Gas-powered leaf blowers are noisy, but they have their uses. Every fall, Robin brings hers to help with leaf removal in areas where raking is difficult or inefficient, or where the metal or plastic tines of rakes would damage plants. As you can see in Figure AU-60, our rock garden presents raking problems: leaves gather between boulders, and among ferns that we want to leave intact through the winter; dwarf evergreens catch leaves under and within them. Blown air frees the leaves from these obstacles, and the plants remain. We use a combination of rakes and the

Figure AU-61. Robin blows the leaves off the beds, and I pick them up immediately with the mulcher.

Figure AU-63. The results of our work show a clean bed ready for winter. Had we left the leaves on the garden, they would have formed thick, wet mats that would have caused crown rot in perennials and prevented shoots from emerging in spring.

leaf blower in the Brick Walk Garden (see Figure AU-61), which doesn't present as many problems for rakes as does the rock garden. First we rake as best we can to gather the bulk of the leaves onto tarps and drag them away. Then Robin follows up with the leaf blower to extricate leaves from within and under shrubs and ground covers. Figure AU-62 shows the garden after we finished with rakes and the blower.

Figures AU-63 to AU-66 show you the entire process of clearing a bed in preparation for winter.

1. Figure AU-63. Part of the Woodland Garden before cutting it back.

2. Figure AU-64. The same area after cutting back all the perennials. Robin is blowing leaves off the evergreen *Phlox stolonifera*.

3. Figure AU-65. Robin is finishing leaf removal with a rake. She gathers tarploads of leaves, which she and Pat drag to a nearby pile.

4. Figure AU-66 (see page 195). That's a Katsura tree we planted in the west meadow years ago. The rake resting against a Japanese tree lilac signals the end of the work for another year.

FIGURE AU-63

FIGURE AU-64

FIGURE AU-65

TREE ASSESSMENT

From late September to early November, as the flowering shrubs and perennials demand less attention, but before outdoor temperatures plummet, my attention shifts to the native trees at the edges of the garden. While the leaves are still on, I assess each tree to see what it adds to or subtracts from the garden. Is it shading too much of the ornamental garden? Does the girth of the tree suggest that its roots are spreading too far into the garden, taking an undue share of water and nutrients? Are the garden plants that we set out under the trees still flourishing, or are they backsliding? In this reassessment, I keep in mind that there are many alternatives to leaving a tree or cutting it down.

HIGH PRUNING

One September during my annual tree assessment, I noticed that branches from maples and black locusts that grow along the west side of a lawn path had grown so far over the path that the grass received no direct sunlight after ten in the morning. That fall, I cut back many of the lower branches to bring more light to the path. In subsequent years I know I'll have to cut down some of the trees as their upper branches spread—or take up the lawn and put down stone.

LEAVE THE TRUNK AS A POST TO SUPPORT A VINE

That same September, I noticed that a 12-inch-diameter thick black locust had grown so tall that it was shading a large area of the mixed border in which it was growing. Rather than cut the locust to the ground, I cut off the top and all the lower branches, leaving a 14-foot-high post in the ground. I girdled its base with a chain saw to prevent sprouting, then trained *Wisteria* 'Aunt Dee' up the post.

CARVE A SCULPTURE IN THE REMAINING TRUNK

One earlier September I discovered that a 16-inch-diameter butternut, a short-lived tree at best, was losing many of its upper branches. Given that there were many other trees in the area, I cut down the butternut, leaving an 8-foot-high trunk. After stripping off the bark, Mary asked our friend Gerry Prozzo, a sculptor, to carve the face of the Green Man, a Druidic symbol of the point where the worlds of man and plants coincide, into the top of the trunk. I treat the carving twice a year with an organic sealant.

CUT ONLY INNER BRANCHES

Last September I was standing under a group of five 14-inch-diameter ash trees, the trunks of which roughly scribed a 30-foot-diameter circle. We had just completed a stone-paved sitting area under the trees when I noticed a thicket of crisscrossing branches overhead. I cut off the inner branches of all five trees to a height of 25 feet, leaving the outer branches intact. In this way I defined a dramatic 25-foot-high, 30-foot-wide open space above our new sitting area.

Cut It Down

There comes a time when a native tree has grown too big, is throwing too much shade or taking too much water and too many nutrients from nearby trees, shrubs, and perennials. That's when I get out the chain saw. I cut up the tree for firewood, and savor the thought of fewer leaves to rake in October.

Too Many Trees Near the House?

To decide whether or not you have too many trees around your home, take a fresh look at them, first from every window and doorway, then from all vantage points from the front, back, and sides of your house. Sometimes trees provide a feeling of separation and privacy between you and your neighbors. Trees can also provide essential shade. The element of privacy might be particularly apparent from the upstairs windows, so you look into the branch of trees rather than your neighbor's windows. On the other hand, you might find that the trees around your house block too much sunlight or beautiful views.

The two most obvious choices are leaving the trees as they are or cutting them down. But in between are many alternatives, all of which involve pruning.

1. HIGH-PRUNING involves cutting off many lower branches to lift the tree's canopy, so when you look out even second-story windows, you see trunk and no branching. The result is a lofty, regal looking tree that almost appears to be floating above your garden. It's best to hire an arborist for this job.

2. THINNING can open up the inner branching of a tree to allow more light to reach the interior of the tree, onto the ground and underplantings, or into your windows, while at the same time defining the tree's architectural branching structure. It's best to consult an arborist, and proceed with care.

3. SHAPING involves pruning or thinning the limbs, ideally in this case between the trunk of the tree and the side of your house. For privacy, leave the branches between the trunk and your neighbor's property so that they arch down, perhaps even to within a foot or two of ground level.

Repairing a Break in a Dry Stone Wall

Figure SW-1. The key to the longevity of a retaining wall is drainage. Keep the water away from its back and base with freely draining crushed stone or gravel. As water-laden soil goes through freeze-thaw or wet-dry cycles, the soil, and thus the wall, shifts and weakens the wall.

There is nothing quite so satisfying as rebuilding a section of tumbled down stone wall. You are participating in a bit of history. And because every stone wall is a reflection of the person who built it, when you set out to repair a section of old stone wall in a thoughtful way, you learn about how someone thought long ago. You are moving stones that he moved. You are digging back into time and sorting out someone else's labor to see what went wrong, what needs doing, what can be done to put things seamlessly right again. And when you are finished, you see the tangible results of a new skill you have developed.

As you look at a broken down section of wall, begin by carefully perusing the tumble itself, then the adjacent intact wall, for pattern and clues that might enable you to read the mind of the builder. You are, after all, trying to understand his style, replicate his work. With knowledge and patience and a keen eye, you will be able to do it. But when we do anything new and unfamiliar, it's always good to go to the experts, and that's what I did. I went to Dan Snow.

Snow is a professional wall builder from southern Vermont. After several years of design study at Pratt Institute in New York City in the 1970s, he went on to many months of apprenticeships in Mexico, Italy, and Scotland, each apprenticeship separated by several years of building dry stone walls, as opposed to mortared walls, in southern Vermont and New Hampshire. He has been practicing his craft for twenty-three years and is one of a handful of dry stone wall builders in America holding certification by the Dry Stone Wallers Association of Great Britain. As a garden designer, I have worked with Dan for years, so naturally I turned to him to learn the basics of repairing a section of fallen wall.

There are two kinds of stone walls: retaining and freestanding. A retaining wall is built into a slope to hold back soil, so as to create a terrace or a level space behind it (see Figure SW-1); freestanding walls are open to the air on both sides and are typically built for enclosure or to establish property boundaries (see Figures SW-2 and SW-3).

Both types of walls tumble at points along their lengths for a variety of reasons. The wall's foundation stones shift due to erosion or uneven settling over decades. Tree roots under the wall grow and expand. The natural freeze-thaw (expansion-contraction) process during the winter causes the soil on which the wall sits to heave and slump. Gaps between stones fill over time with moisture-retaining organic matter, which in turn freezes and thaws and unsettles a wall. Or perhaps you've backed into the wall with your new car.

SORTING OUT THE STONE THAT TUMBLED DOWN

One of the first things you need to do is clear away all the tumbled-down stones until you come to sound construction. As you sort stones, don't throw them atop one another; try to keep the patina of age on each stone intact by handling them with reasonable care so they don't become scratched and chipped. The goal of your work is to seamlessly knit the repair into the existing wall.

As you clear the tumble, leave any large base stones that are in appropriate places. Sort the remaining stones into different piles according to their roles in your finished wall: heavy stones with right angles for corners; cap stones, which need to be as wide as the wall; long through stones, which need to be the width of the wall; tiny shards and bits, for hearting (stuffing); and face stones, which will make the repaired section look just like the old wall. If it's clear that you will need additional stone, look for out-of-the-way walls on your own property as sources. (In most parts of the country, it is against the law to remove stones from a boundary wall between you and a neighbor's property. As Mr. Frost wrote, "Good fences make good neighbors.")

As you sort out and move heavy stones, and later begin to repair your wall, Snow says you should take advantage of gravity and physics. Rather than lift a stone, flip it end over end, directing the topple when the stone is on end to where you will need the stone. Rolling, flipping, and spinning are always preferable to lifting. Facilitate sliding or moving large stones by placing a piece of plywood on pipes or wooden rollers, then getting the stones onto the plywood. You can then roll the stone to the wall rather than lift it, then use a board ramp to help you roll the stone up onto the wall.

CHOOSING WHERE TO BEGIN

Once you have the stones sorted, remove all the soil and organic matter from the base of the wall by digging down 6 to 8 inches below ground level. You want to bury at least some of the bulk of the base stones. If you decide to leave any of the existing base stones in place, just dig around them. If you are mending a break in a retaining wall, remove the soil behind the section you need to repair. Excavate 18 to 24 inches back from the sound wall, and remove the soil. As you build up the height of the wall, fill the void with scrap stone. It will improve drainage and thereby reduce the chances that you will have to repair that section of wall again in a few years.

Now you are ready to start laying stone. If your repairs involve the corner of a wall, start your repair work there. It's easier to work away from a finished corner than toward it. If your repairs involve stone steps, start there, being certain to knit the steps and the adjacent walls together as you go up.

SPECIFICS OF LAYING WALL STONE

Start by laying the largest stones in your stockpile in the base of the wall (see Figures SW-2 and SW-3). Once you have the base laid, you can build the front and back faces of the wall at the same pace, filling in the center as you go. (A freestanding wall has two faces that have to look good; a retaining wall has only one exposed face.) As you begin to build a face, constantly refer to the sound sections of the wall so the mend mirrors the existing wall as much as possible. Place the lowest facing stones atop the base stones, then step back to see if the look replicates the existing wall. If you've got a good match, use smaller pieces to pack under the face stones to hold them firmly in place.

Dan Snow stresses how important it is to continually develop a good surface to build on. That means that you are hearting (stuffing) and building up level planes for the next stones all the time. If you are constantly creating a level base for the next stones, wall building becomes an inviting process rather than a seemingly endless series of difficulties.

Lay stones along the whole section of wall you're repairing rather than looking for the right stone for one spot at a time. This increases the likelihood that you will find an appropriate place for the next stone you pick up. And avoid using the laying surface as a storage shelf for unset stones. They will distract you from seeing all the possible places for the next stone.

Figure SW-2. Slightly slanting the rocks back into the center of a freestanding wall strengthen it. The largest stones in a wall belong below ground level, where they form a sturdy base.

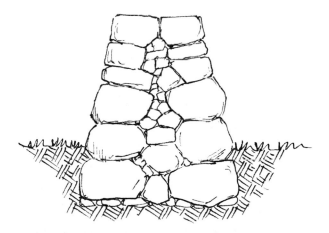

Figure SW-3. The batter is the backward lean in both faces of a freestanding wall. It ensures that the wall's center of gravity is well within the wall, where it can stabilize it.

How Stone Should Be Bedded

Bedding is the process of setting the stones into place. The one rule that Dan Snow and other dry wallers insist upon is that you set the longest dimension of each stone perpendicular to the length of the wall rather than parallel to it. Choose the best-looking end of the stone to face outward. The tail—the end of the stone that will be buried in the wall—points toward the center. By setting the length of the stone into the wall, with its upper surface as level as possible, you knit interior and exterior, back and front, to create an interrelated whole. By setting stone so that its upper surface is as level as possible, you establish a stable base for the next course. Steady each stone before moving on to the next stone. Once laid, a stone should not move when you try to shift it with your hand left or right, back or forth.

Joints: How Stones Relate to One Another

Wallers always keep in mind this rule: one stone need lie atop two; two stones need lie atop one. This ensures that all the face stones are bonded together, and there are no weak seams created by long vertical joints. The interior of the wall also needs to be knit together, so the tail of stones coming from the A side lie atop the tail of stones coming from the B side. Finally, place the largest surface area of each stone within the wall: the more area, the more friction, which means stronger gripping of one rock to another.

Batter

Batter is the angle, or taper, of the exterior face of the wall as it leans back ever so gradually toward the center of the wall as its height increases (see Figures SW-2 and SW-3). When repairing a wall, you should match the batter of the new to old. Batter, which is central to a long-lasting wall, is sometimes created by tilting the stones down into the center of the wall. Batter can also be achieved by setting each course back just a bit, typically 1 inch per foot of wall height. For example, over 4 feet of height, the face of the wall recedes about 4 inches from plumb, bottom to top. This ensures that the thrust of the wall is inward, and the weight of the wall is centralized (see Figure SW-3).

Hearting

To prevent slippage or subsidence due to internal hollows, you need to keep the interior of the wall firmly and fully stuffed. Hearting, which is that stuffing, consists of stones from a sliver up to 8 inches that are hidden in the interior of the wall (see Figures SW-2 and SW-3). It could be the rubble that results from trimming and shaping stone as you rebuild the wall, or the hearting from other old walls on your property. Snow says he would never use pea stone, gravel, or sand as hearting: "What you can pour in with a shovel can pour back out over time."

THROUGH STONES

Through stones are as wide as a wall is thick. They are placed at random heights along the length of a wall and extend through the full thickness of it, thereby tying the two faces together. Don't be tempted to put a long, flat stone with its length along the face of the wall just for looks. Lay it across the wall for stability.

CAPPING A WALL

Cap stones run along the top of a wall and are ideally as wide as the wall is thick. The goal of any wall builder is to create a wall capping that is solid enough to stay in place if children climb on it. You want the cap stones in the repaired section to match those of the intact sections of wall. Safety, as well as longevity and aesthetics, are the central qualities of good capping, so make certain that the underside of the cap stones touch the hearting and facing stones below it so as not to rock or shift.

BACKFILLING A RETAINING WALL

As you build up the face and heart of a retaining wall, you also need to bring up the back of the wall. Because the backfilling and hearting will not be visible, you can be rougher in your construction style, but don't take shortcuts. Set every stone, then heart it with smaller stone, and be certain to lay plenty of stone well back into the excavated section of the soil behind the wall (see Figure SW-1). When you get within a foot or so of the existing grade level, lay permeable land-scape fabric atop the backfilling (see Figure SW-1). Once you complete your repairs, shovel topsoil onto the fabric so the soil meets the top of the repaired section as well as the intact wall in a similar way. The fabric is there to prevent the soil from leaching down into the crevices of the wall stones, where it would fill the gaps between stones and, during the winter, start the freeze-thaw expansion-contraction process that weakens the wall.

Avoid working in the rain when the ground and stones are slippery. Think about how to move heavy stones efficiently and safely; it's an absorbing challenge. Step back now and again to take stock, and notice the way light and shadow, curved and straight lines, and all the shades of gray play across your wall. Enjoy the fact that, in repairing a wall, you are following the lead of someone you don't know; there is good satisfaction in that anonymity, in that matching of new to old, of you to a stranger. Above all, be patient with yourself and the rocks, and listen to your body; it will tell you when to stop.

CHECKLIST

- Bring in the outdoor furniture, removable gates, and garden ornaments and store them under cover.
- Dismantle pots planted with annuals; compost the soilless mix and the plants themselves. The soilless mix can also go directly onto beds.
- Store terra-cotta pots over the winter in a dry place.
- Start leaf raking the first day they fall. Stay on top of this chore and it won't become unmanageable.
- Drain the hoses and hang them up.
- Cut back and compost herbaceous perennials that, unlike perennial grasses, won't look good in the garden through the winter.
- Remove trees and shrubs that are ailing or have grown out of scale and create too much shade.
- Assess all trees and shrubs with an eye to which ones should be removed or pruned.
- Cut perennials that dry well for winter bouquets: hydrangea blooms, perennial grasses, and *Sedum* (now *Hylotelephium*) *spectabile* flower heads.
- Save potted plants that dry well, such as blood red *Pennisetum setaceum*. Allowed to dry in the pots, they will look good all winter long.
- Plant bulbs.
- Divide plants that need it, water them well, and mulch them; take no shortcuts with fall transplanting.
- Reduce the size of plants that have gotten too big. We take great pieces of root systems from the edges of ornamental grasses and Joe Pye weed and give them away. We take up whole root systems of plants such as Siberian iris, which die in the middle and compost the center portion.
- Divide peonies and *Sanguinaria canadensis* 'Flore Pleno'. This is the only time of year to divide these.
- Uproot excess freely seeding perennials, such as *Alchemilla mollis*, *Heliopsis helianthoides* 'Summer Sun', and *Astrantia major* 'Rosea', that have spread far and wide.
- Remove *Dennstaedtia punctilobula* (hay-scented fern) and other aggressive plants that have insinuated themselves into inappropriate spots in the garden.
- Keep pots of tender annual herbs such as oregano, basil, and parsley under cover to extend their usefulness for a week or two, or until a deep frost kills them off.

CHANGING LAWN SHAPE FOR BETTER GARDEN COHERENCE

You can easily revise your garden design with a straight-nosed spade. I edit our garden with one all the time. In about three hours this past September, I changed an amorphous level lawn surrounded by perennials into an oval green panel. This strong new shape provides the visual anchor this area lacked. See your own lawn as a piece of paper and your straight-nosed spade as a drawing pencil, and there's no telling what changes you can make in the name of coherence and handsome proportion in your garden.

Too often, gardeners dig beds at the edge of or within grassed areas without paying attention to the shape of the remaining lawn or the proportion of bed to lawn. The result is often a 3-foot-wide perennial bed at the edge of a 70-foot-long lawn, or a 10-foot-long curvy bed in a 100-foot-long sea of green. No matter how we plant these beds, they look wrong.

Bed and lawn shapes need to be developed in unison, so that the two are visually related, in proportion, and feel appropriate. Square, rectangular, and circular panels of lawn look best on flat areas. On sloping areas, curving lawn paths of a uniform width that mimic the shape of a meandering stream look best. With a straight-nosed spade, lawn comes up easily in 1-inch-thick sods, so the problem of incoherent and ill-proportioned lawn and bed shapes can be easily remedied.

Before I get into the nuts and bolts of this idea, go into your garden and make a simple sketch of your lawn, or just the back section behind the house.

USE DRIP LINES OF TREES OR SHRUB BORDERS TO PROVIDE LOGICAL EDGES

When determining the shape of the lawn in any area of your garden, you are, by default, determining the front edge of any garden bed that abuts the lawn. To make the lawn/bed edge logical and relate it to the larger picture, look around to nearby walls, hedges, buildings, or established beds and lawns for clues. Major trees in your garden and their drip lines—that is, the outer tips of the tree's branches—often provide good clues.

One day years ago I was at the far end of our garden looking closely at an eighty-year-old standard apple tree that was growing in the midst of a free-form lawn with beds planted around its perimeter. I realized that there was no coherence between the circular form of the tree, the curvy edge of the beds, and the free-form shape of the lawn. After considering a number of shapes for the lawn, none of which were suggested by existing features of the garden, I looked up to see that the circular outline of the apple tree could be repeated on the ground in a circular panel of lawn. I measured the radius of the tree's outline: 30 feet. I loosely tied one end of a 50-foot rope to the base of the tree, then, holding the rope's far end, walked around the perimeter of the lawn. After trying a variety of radii, I settled on a 40-foot radius, because it would enable me to remove as little lawn as possible yet still make 300 degrees of a circle (see Figures LS-1 and LS-2). (The remaining 60 degrees would be squared off at the north edge, where circular lawn met square bed.)

I marked the circumference of the circle with thirty or so bamboo stakes, then I cut the edge with the straight-nosed spade and lifted the excess sod. By planting new perennials and transplanting others into the newly opened spaces, I changed the garden/lawn edge to mimic the circular shape of the tree canopy, thereby relating tree, lawn, and beds through one idea—the circle (see Figure LS-2).

NEARBY FEATURES AS CUES TO NEW LAWN SHAPES

Sometimes obvious clues such as a large tree aren't there to help you visualize or generate appropriate new lawn shapes. Recently I was reassessing the lawn shape in our back garden. It roughly followed the outline of a grand piano and as such made no sense in relation to linear adjacent features such as stone walls, the end of the barn, and an arborvitae hedge. I wanted the shape of the lawn to be simpler and stronger, to provide a strong visual center for the area. I also wanted to create a coherent garden picture where lawn, beds, walls, building, and hedge were parallel or perpendicular to one another.

I measured the longest length of the existing lawn, following a line that was parallel with a stone wall 15 feet away and perpendicular to the end of the barn, 30 feet away. The lawn was just over 40 feet long. Then I measured the width of the lawn at various points along its length. I found that an 18-foot width would enable me to remove as little grass as possible, yet be able to create a strong geometric shape within the existing level lawn. Deciding to bring the shape of a half circle into the picture, in part to echo the circle under the apple tree, I used bamboo stakes to mark a 9-foot-radius semicircle at either end of the 40-foot by 18-foot lawn panel (see Figures LS-3 and LS-4).

I then lifted the lawn outside the lines and stakes, added compost to the newly exposed soil, and planted the new open areas. I also added large stepping-stones to two existing walkways so that the geometrically shaped lawn was literally linked to the paths.

Joining Previously Unrelated Island Beds for Greater Coherence

Changing lawn edges can also bring unrelated island beds set within a large level lawn into a sound relationship with one another. For example, if you have five island beds in your lawn that bear no particular visual relationship to one another, take a close look at how the gaps of lawn between two or three of them can be taken up to create one single shape that is related to nearby features: another major bed, a lawn, a stone path, or a nearby building. The open soil can then be planted to make one large bed that has greater unity and impact.

Make a sketch, drawing two or three of these beds into one, and you might see a pattern emerge. For example, in one garden I worked in, we joined three beds into one, which gave us the idea to join two other nearby beds into one; where there had been five, there were now two. At that point we saw that with the little effort it would take to remove a bit more sod, we could create a large section of lawn between the two new beds that was semicircular, thereby relating the two large beds we'd created.

Making the Most of Transitions Between Garden Areas

There is another important use to which this idea of changing lawn shapes can be put: transitions. Many times a narrow section of lawn joins two other much larger areas of lawn with gardens within or around their perimeters. The result is a lawn shaped like an hourglass. By using lawn as the transition between two large areas of lawn, you lose the opportunity to create a clear sense of leaving one area and entering another. By taking up the lawn in that tight center of the hourglass and using stepping-stones, gravel, cut stones, brick—in fact, any material other than lawn—then further marking the transition with an arbor or a gate, you create drama, surprise, and a strong feeling of arrival.

Here's an example from our own garden, one that relates back to the old standard apple tree. Several years ago the free-form panel of lawn under the apple tree segued into a 15-foot-wide, 20-foot-long panel of lawn that gently sloped down between two planted beds to a post-and-beam gazebo (see Figure LS-1). Given the beauty of the gazebo and the drama of its setting at the edge of the meadow and with views beyond, I wanted to make more of the transition from the lawn around the apple tree to the lawn in front of the gazebo. I took up the 15-foot by 20-foot lawn connector and planted five pairs of 8-foot-high purple-leaved beech saplings, to form a 20-foot-long, 8-foot-high and -wide tunnel of beech trees. To create flat steps down the gentle slope, I set five 8-foot-long black locust posts as risers and pea stone as the surface on which to walk. Now,

AFTER

E Sran

Figure LS-1. Before: The ill-defined lawn between our apple tree and adjacent beds did not relate all the parts into a coherent whole. In fact, arbitrarily shaped lawns tend to separate areas that should be visually related to one another.

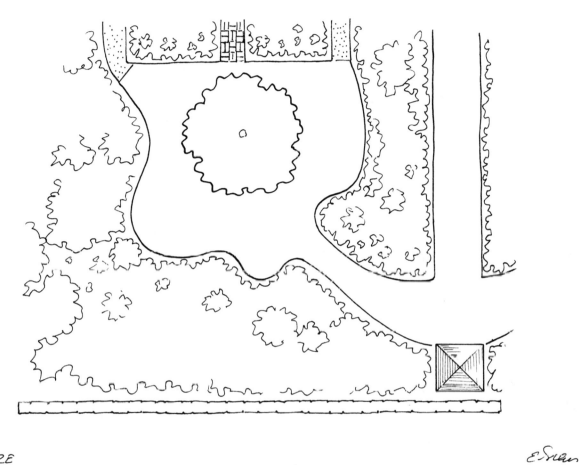

BEFORE

Figure LS-2. After: Reshaping the lawn by using a uniform radius drew the various beds at the edge of the lawn into a new relationship with one another. The circular lawn shape reflects the circular canopy of the apple tree.

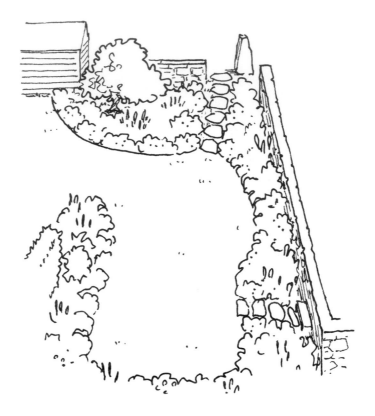

Figure LS-3. Before: The shape of the lawn we used to have bore no relationship to the important walls at the edges of the garden. Furthermore, using lawn for the narrow transition into the area did not underpin the idea of leaving one area and entering another.

Figure LS-4. (Opposite) After: The new ellipse-shaped lawn relates to the lines of the stone walls, and the curves at the ends of the lawn add grace to the shape. The lawn has become positive space, not negative space

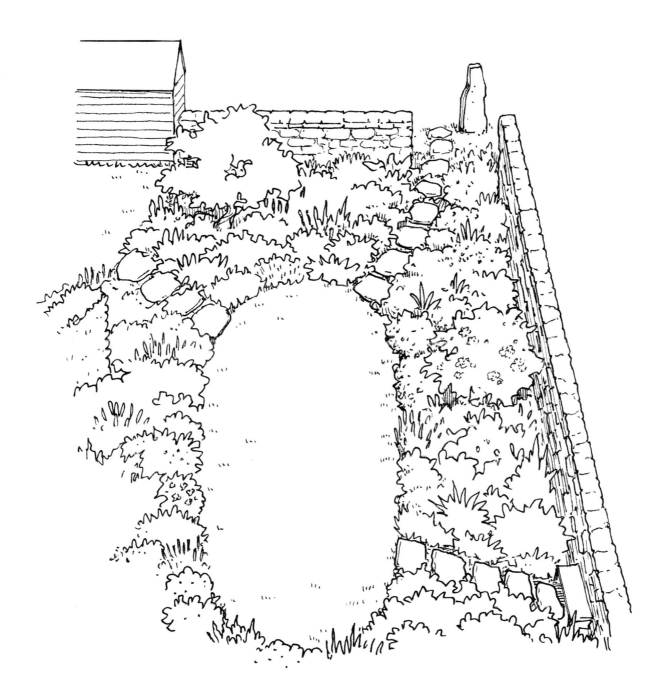

when you walk from the lawn under the apple tree toward the gazebo, the tunnel frames its entrance (see figure W-31 on page 47); thereby turning the previously indistinct transition area into a dramatic garden image. When leaving the gazebo, you enter the tunnel, which frames a view of the trunk of the apple tree and its muscular branching system.

Now, look closely at the sketch you did of your own lawn, and you may find points of transition where the lawn narrows between two garden areas. Once you take up this lawn, look in all directions for clues as to how to make the transition special. If a cut-stone path leads onto the same panel of lawn, lay formal cut stones to make the transition. If your house is brick, you could lay old brick in the transition zone; if your garden is relaxed and casual, use gravel, pea stone, or field-stones. Be generous enough with the dimensions of the paved transition area to accommodate large planted pots, a garden ornament, or a beautiful jardiniere, adding further visual interest to the transition. Consider a gate, an arbor, or a pergola for the transition area as well, and densely planting shrubs and perennials on either side of it to obscure all but a narrow and thereby enticing view of the next garden. If the lawn slopes in this transition zone, build steps to form a series of level and safe surfaces as you make the transition between garden areas.

The key to all this is, of course, your good sense of proportion and line, but the actual work rests on the straight-nosed spade. This tool typically has a rectangular blade $7\frac{1}{2}$ inches wide and 11 inches long set on a 32-inch stout shaft with a D- or T-shaped handle. The major difference between the blade of this spade and that of the pointed, curved shovel you use most of the time is that this blade is straight. Cut a lawn edge with this tool, well sharpened, and you get a fine straight or broadly curving edge. Cut it with your curved shovel, the one you use to plant shrubs, and you create a scalloped, ragged line.

What you will find if you become a student of lawn shape change—a student of line, proportion, unity, and coherence in your garden—is that you can make hugely satisfying changes in your garden with remarkably little work.

PURCHASING TOPSOIL

Now and again you may need to buy topsoil to build up the quality of soil in your garden. The typical load for delivery to a residence is about 6 to 7 cubic yards in size and is delivered in a two-axle dump truck; 16-cubic-yard loads are delivered in a three-axle dump truck. One cubic yard (27 cubic feet) covers an area 10 feet by 10 feet to a depth of 4 inches.

If you need topsoil, ask for the name of suppliers at a reputable garden center, or do research on the web at local.com. There you can type in the name of your state, then "topsoil suppliers," and you'll get a pre-screened list of reputable businesses. If you will be using the topsoil directly in planted beds, look for suppliers of soil that has been premixed with compost and other organic matter; it is gorgeous stuff. It will cost more but will save you a great deal of work.

Once you've located a supplier or two, ask to see their topsoil piles. If the owner refuses, go somewhere else. Over twenty-five years of installing gardens across the Northeast, I have seen some truly miserable material being sold under the name of "topsoil," as well as number of things that shouldn't have been there in the first place: quackgrass rhizomes and the roots of other invasive grasses and plants, wood chips, whole sods of grass that had been growing on top of the mound in the supply yard, rocks, weeds as tall as I am, and small chunks of asphalt and concrete. A general contractor with whom I once worked had an entire load of clay dug up from the bottom of a pond and delivered to the job site as topsoil; a potter could have thrown pots with it.

Be sure to see the soil before ordering it. If, on arrival at a supply yard, you see a pile of topsoil covered with weeds, go elsewhere. Otherwise, look closely at the pile for any of the undesirable materials I've mentioned. Also, dig your hand into the pile; feel the soil's weight, and get a sense of how open and fertile it is. Ask the supplier where the soil came from. If he answers "farmland," ask if the farmer used herbicides on his land. If so, opt out. Once you have found a reputable supplier, ask about cost per cubic yard and delivery fees.

Here's what to look for in quality topsoil:

- TEXTURE: Wet some of the soil and rub it between your fingers. You're looking for a balance between gritty, sandy particles; soapy or silky particles of silt; and sticky, fine clay particles. If any one texture is clearly predominant, the soil is out of balance. If all three are about equal, you are looking at good loamy topsoil.
- STRUCTURE: Work a sample of the soil

into a lump on the palm of your hand. Then press into the center of the lump with your fingers. The lump should break into crumblike particles. If you can't form a lump with it, there's too much sand; if the lump doesn't break down when you poke it with your finger, it has too much clay.

- ORGANIC MATTER: You want topsoil with a lot of organic matter. Black or dark brown soil has a high percentage. Gray and light gray soils have very little.
- SALTS: Look closely at the topsoil pile in the supplier's yard for thin white crystals, or even a crust of them, that have formed on the dry surface of the pile. Crystals indicate an excessive amount of salts. Don't buy such soil.
- pH: Ask the supplier for the soil pH, the standard measure of acidity or alkalinity. You're looking for soil with a pH between 5.5 and 7.5. Anything above or below that is too extreme to support healthy plant growth.

Plan ahead for delivery. Select a place the driver can reach easily without backing over your lawn. Preferably, the soil should be dumped close to the edge of your driveway. To ease cleanup, lay down large tarps where the driver can dump the load. Make sure there are no overhead wires, tree limbs, or other obstructions that might be damaged; the dump body of a 7-yard dump truck rises 14 to 16 feet or so above the ground. Once the delivery is complete, cover the soil immediately with tarps and weight them down with stones. You want to prevent rain from soaking the soil before you spread it, and weed seeds from blowing into the soil and germinating.

Appendix

HIRING HELP IN THE GARDEN

Over the years, we have hired skilled, semi-skilled, or unskilled labor to help with specific jobs in the garden:

- Lay a brick walk
- Mow the lawn in our absence
- Cut down major trees inside the garden (an arborist who knows how to climb trees with a chain saw in hand)
- Take up large areas of sod to turn a previously lawn-covered area into a perennial garden
- Help weed before an open-garden day

Here's how to find the right person for the job.

EVALUATE YOUR GARDEN

Go from area to area in your garden and make brief notes of the jobs that are required. As you evaluate each area, keep in mind that you don't have to hire a full-time or even part-time gardener. Maybe you just need help now and again from skilled or semiskilled people. Ask yourself:

- Which jobs are repetitive and could be done by someone you trained or who has the basic skills necessary for the job?

- Which jobs do you find rewarding and which tedious?
- What jobs need to be done weekly? Monthly? Yearly? Maybe you could hire someone to help with, or take over, the entire spring cleanup of the lawns and beds, and do all the cutting back and leaf raking in fall, and you do everything else.
- How much time do you spend mowing the lawn? Is that a job you could hire out? What would the costs be? If you hire a lawn service, limit their responsibility to the lawn. Don't let them convince you they know how to prune and weed. Before hiring, ask about their attitude toward using chemicals on lawns (a crucial question if you have children).
- If your trees and shrubs need pruning now and again, can you hire a trained arborist? (Make sure they don't use electric hedge shears and trim your shrubs into little mounds.)
- Can you hire someone to plant several trees, shrubs, or perennials?
- Can you benefit from the advice of a trained horticulturist or knowledgeable garden maintenance person?

Where to Find Help

- Ask neighbors or friends who have terrific gardens if they know anyone who can help with specific jobs.
- Contact a regional horticultural college to see if students are looking for work.
- Call a garden designer or highly recommended landscaper and ask for his or her recommendations.
- Go to the best garden center or nursery in the area and ask the owner for recommendations.

Whom to Hire

- Once you have a short list of applicants, ask for the names and phone numbers of the last three people who hired the applicant. This should result in three phone calls and perhaps three visits to their gardens. (Asking for references will elicit only that person's successes.)
- When calling for references, ask if the applicant is willing to take direction, yet shows initiative.
- If you are interviewing for maintenance help, know that people have different attitudes toward detail, work at different paces, and have different expectations regarding breaks and lunch hours, et cetera. Ask specific questions about these issues.
- Trust your intuition. Imagine that you will work next to this person in the garden. Would you look forward to spending time talking with this person as you worked? Does the person inspire confidence?
- If you are considering hiring a garden maintenance firm that offers a broad range of services, ask if they are affiliated with state or area nursery or landscape associations—and, if so, which ones. If it seems appropriate given the size of the organization, contact the organization to discuss the applicant.
- Work out a realistic budget and keep it in mind as you inquire about hourly rates.

After Hiring

- Offer the job based on a trial period of six weeks or so. Stress that this trial period is in the interest of employer and employee.
- During the trial period, be aware of how employees use tools and equipment. Are they careful and respectful? Do they seem knowledgeable? Are you comfortable with their pace? Do they work with confidence? When you ask them questions, do they provide clear and substantive answers?
- Accept that people you hire for long-term work might do things differently than you do. If the difference is negligible, let it go. Keep your priorities straight. A cordial working relationship is more important than trying to make someone over in your image.
- If you find people who know what they're doing, whom you like to have around, who show up on time and work at a steady pace throughout the day, pay them well and keep them happy. They are worth their weight in gold.

Gardens and the Drip Lines of Houses

*(Excerpted from **Your House, Your Garden**)*

Your house may not have gutters along its eaves, so rainwater runs off or snow cascades onto plantings below. The falling water splashes mulch or soil onto house siding, discoloring it or causing it to rot prematurely, or it damages nearby plants. Heavy snow can break off branches and sometimes entire plants.

Walk along the eave sides of your house and you will see an erosion line, or drip line, on the ground. When an inch of rain falls, 1,500 gallons of water cascade off a typical 2,500-square-foot roof onto the plantings below.

There are a variety of solutions that you can employ to handle problems associated with drip lines. Before considering any of the solutions below, however, check the soil along the drip lines to see if it is compacted and has little tilth or openness. Also have the soil tested for lead (from sloughed-off old paint) and for pH, especially if you live in an area beset by acid rain. Unlike other areas of your garden that receive more evenly dispersed rainfall, the soil under the drip line and a foot or two out from it has often been leached of; nutrients little organic matter remains.

Rather than reinvigorate the soil between the foundation and 6 inches beyond the drip line, excavate it. In parts of North America where 15 to 25 inches of rain falls in a year, excavate down 6 inches in that area. Lay water-permeable landscape fabric in the resulting trench, then cover it with 6 inches of $^3/_8$-inch pea stone or other small, rounded stone indigenous to your area that looks attractive (see Figure DL-1). (Avoid crushed stone; it is often unattractive and has an engineered look. And avoid large, flat stones, because such a surface does not break up water into droplets. Water splashes off the flat surfaces and onto the siding of the house.) When water falls on small stones, droplets disperse, causing no harm or mess to house or plants. Once the small stones are in place, you can amend the soil beyond the backfilled trench, and plant as you normally would.

In areas of North America where the rainfall is more than 25 inches a year, or in the Southwest, with its periodic torrential downpours, huge volumes of water often cascade off a roof. What I did at our own home in southern Vermont, where we typically get 44 inches of rain a year, and sometimes more than 2 inches in a single storm, was to excavate 14 to 16 inches down against the foundation to a point 6 inches out from it. The trench ended at a low spot at the far end of the house where it could drain onto the lawn. I lined the trench with landscape fabric, then heavy-gauge plastic sheeting, then spread a 2-inch-thick layer of $^3/_8$-inch pea stone in the lined trench. I set 4-inch-diameter perforated pipe (holes facing down) atop the pea stone, frequently checking with a spirit level to be sure that the pipe was gently sloping so it would drain. I then filled the remaining space with the rest of the pea stone.

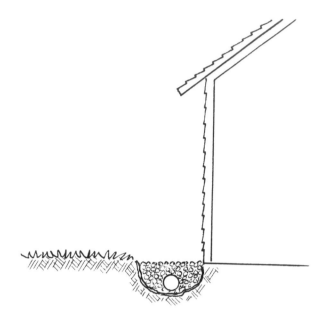

Figure DL-1. Small stones disperse rainwater dripping from a roof edge so the water does not splash onto the siding of the house, and PVC pipe hidden within the ³/₈-inch pea stone carries the water away from the house.

Dormers, and especially roof valleys—where two wings of a house meet at right angles, concentrate rainwater coming off a roof. Below such valleys, you'll need larger rounded stones set almost a foot out from the drip line to withstand heavier, more concentrated downpours. I use 3- to 6-inch river rocks set several inches into the pea stone in such a corner (see Figure DL-2).

If this drainage system is not screened by shrubs and perennials, and lawn runs right up to its edge, there are a number of attractive ways to make a low-maintenance transition between lawn and pea stone. Set a 12- to 16-inch-wide band tightly fitting pieces of cut stone or irregularly shaped flat sandstone, limestone, or mica

schist between the lawn and the pea stone. If you fit the ends of those stones tightly together, the lawn will not creep between them. And the stones will provide a stable, level surface for lawn mower wheels, so you can easily maintain the edge where lawn meets stone.

If you live where it snows and have a smooth roof off of which snow cascades onto shrubs and trees planted along the eaves of your house, plant only tough, deep-rooted perennials here. These plants die back in winter and can survive under mounds of snow for months on end. On the north and east sides of your house, combinations of shade-tolerant hostas, ferns, epimedium, astilbe, and tough ground covers such as periwinkle (*Vinca minor* 'Golden Bowles') or bigroot geranium (*Geranium macrorrhizum*) will do fine. On the south or west sides, plant daylilies, helenium, asters, Siberian iris, Shasta daisies, or other deep-rooted, sun-loving perennials.

If you want to plant shrubs along a drip line where snow damage is a problem, and you don't want unsightly triangular wooden shelters for winter protection, plant at least 18 inches out from the drip line. Choose shrubs with flexible, not brittle, branches or with a prostrate habit. And choose plants that bloom on new wood, so if you have to prune back damaged twigs and branches, the shrub will have time between early spring and midsummer to generate new growth on which it will flower. As a rule of thumb, any shrub that blooms after July 4 blooms on new wood.

SHRUBS WITH FLEXIBLE BRANCHES

Andrachne colchica
Chamaecyparis pisifera **hybrids**
Cotoneaster
Forsythia 'Arnold Dwarf'
Fothergilla gardenii
Kerria japonica
Leucothoe fontanesiana 'Compacta' or 'Nana'
Rhus aromatica 'Gro-low'
Salix purpurea 'Nana'
Sasa veitchii
Spirea
Symphoricarpos × *chenaultii* 'Hancock'
Taxus × *media* 'Densiformis'
Xanthoriza simplicissima

SHRUBS WITH A PROSTRATE GROWTH HABIT

Cornus canadensis
Cytisus decumbens
Forsythia viridissima 'Bronxensis'
Gaultheria prucumbens
Ground cover roses
Juniperus communis
Leucothoe fontanesiana 'Compacta'
Linnaea borealis
Mahonia aquifolium
Microbiotta decussata
Paxistima canbyi
Picea abies 'Nidiformis'
Sarcococca hookeriana humilis

SHRUBS THAT BLOOM ON NEW WOOD

Buddleia davidii
Caryopteris × *clandonensis*
Clerodendrum trichotomum
Clethra alnifolia
Diervilla sessilifolia 'Butterfly'
Hypericum
Lespedeza bicolor
Polygonum aubertii (fleecevine)
Rose
Sorbaria sorbifolia

QUESTIONS TO ASK YOURSELF

- Does my house have drains around the foundation?
- Does water drip off my roof and splash onto plants and house siding?
- What is the nature and condition of the soil along the drip lines? Is it gravelly and well drained or clayey and slow draining?
- Have nutrients been leached out of the soil by excessive water?
- Is the soil along the drip lines wetter, so drought-tolerant plants won't grow well?
- Does snow cascade off the roof, so shrubs won't grow well? Or does snow simply blow off and gather within the shrubs' branches?
- What small indigenous stones will look natural along the drip line in my region?

EXTENDED ROOF OVERHANGS AND RESULTING DRY AREAS BELOW

On many modern homes, roof overhangs can extend out from walls as much as 2 to 3 feet. This broad space near the house remains extremely dry throughout the year and shady throughout the day, making it difficult if not impossible for plants to flourish. You can install a drip irrigation system that won't spray up onto the house walls the way a pop-up irrigation system will, but even with properly aimed irrigation heads, the soil will dry out, especially in winter in cold areas of the country when the system is turned off.

The most effective treatment I have found for an area under an extensive overhang is a maintenance path between the house foundation and the plantings, outside the drip line. Excavate 3 to 6 inches of soil from the foundation to about 6 inches beyond the drip line. Lay down landscape fabric, then cover it with a 2- to 3-inch layer of 1½-inch crushed stone. Top-dress it with 1 to 2 inches of ⅜-inch pea stone. If you live in the arid Southwest, indigenous gravel could come right up to the foundation.

In parts of the country where rainfall is even, not torrential and sporadic, plant gardens 6 inches out from the drip line to help soften the exposed foundation, thereby settling your home into the landscape.

If you live in a modern home with simple geometric lines, it might be preferable to install a black anodized aluminum, steel, or cedar edge set 6 inches out from the drip line, and plant lawn right up to it. This creates a sleek, simple line that emphasizes clean architecture. Your gardens could be situated around the outer perimeter of the lawn rather than close to the house.

DRAINAGE OFF THE ELL ROOF

Water sheets off a roof—that is, rain falls on a roof, then drains from it in a sheet the length of the roof. When two sections of roof come together at right angles, as they do in an ell, the parts of the roof near the intersection drain to a common point, the valley, down which the water runs in a stream. If your home is not or cannot be equipped with gutters, this stream creates a drainage problem. Without some accommoda-

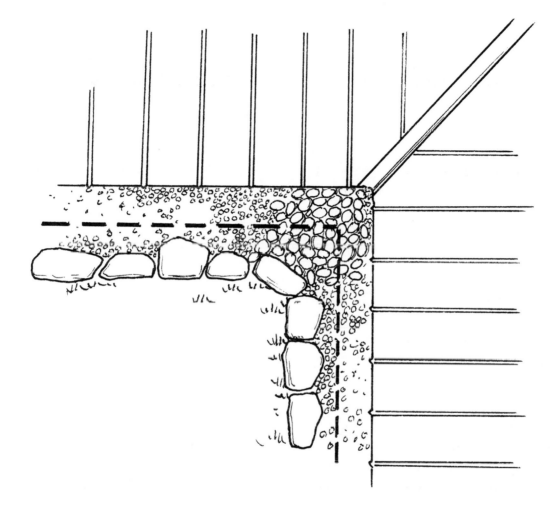

tion for the force of this water falling 10 to 20 feet, considerable erosion takes place.

Most homes built over the last twenty-five years or so have what is called a curtain drain built against the exterior of the base of the foundation. Stout PVC pipe is set into freely draining crushed rock that typically extends from the foundation wall out about 24 to 36 inches. This system collects and carries off some rainwater falling from the roof, but more importantly it carries groundwater away from the house. Check with your builder or the previous owner to see whether a curtain drain was installed. Also try to determine where it drains (the end of the pipe should be at a low point about 20 to 50 feet away from the house). If you don't find it, you need to ask the builder, "Where does the pipe come to daylight?"

Curtain drains can become clogged if the small grate set at the end of the drain falls out or is damaged by string trimming, lawn mowing, heavy equipment, or the force of water running through it. The grate is there to keep small animals such as chipmunks from scurrying up the pipe, nesting there in dry weather, and obstructing the eventual flow of water.

To determine whether the system is draining water away from your foundation, dig down 1 to 3 feet or so in the area just below the roof valley until you expose landscape fabric, which contractors usually use to cover the crushed rock of the curtain drain. Run a hose set on top of the fabric, then explore low spots, banks, or slopes 20 feet or more from the house, listening for the sound of flowing water. If you find where the drainpipe comes to daylight, you know that the curtain drain is working, and you can check to see that the grate is set into the end of the pipe.

If the soil under the roof valleys is badly eroded, excavate all the soil 3 feet or so beyond the intersecting foundation walls under the valley and all the way down to the landscape fabric of the curtain drain. Backfill the hole with 1½-inch crushed stone, then top-dress with more attractive 3- to 4-inch round river rocks. In this way you can ensure that the excessive water draining from a valley does not destroy nearby gardens. Do not place flat stones atop the river rocks, because they spray water back onto the house siding; smaller river rocks break up water into droplets that aren't as damaging. Use a row of flat rocks or steel edging to separate garden soil or beds from the river rocks (see Figure DL-2).

If you live in an especially dry area of the country, place a collecting barrel under the valley and atop any of the above stony surfaces. The barrel will fill and overflow quickly in a rain, and excess water will drain away. After the storm, you'll have a barrelful of water for garden use. Another solution, especially attractive on homes of modern or Far Eastern design, that the Japanese employ is to hang a chain from the lowest point of the valley to within a bed of river rocks. When it rains, water trails down the chain links, providing the delightful sound of falling water.

Bibliography

SOURCES FOR GARDENING AND MAINTENANCE INFORMATION

BOOKS

Aust, Tracy DiSabato. *The Well-Tended Perennial Garden*. Portland, OR: Timber Press, 1998 (ISBN 0881924148).

Berry, Susan, and Steve Bradley. *The Low-Maintenance Garden: A Complete Guide to Designs, Plants and Techniques for Easy-Care Gardens*. Ontario, Canada: Firefly, 2000 (ISBN 1552095142).

Cebenko, Jill, and Deborah Martin, ed. *Insect, Disease and Weed ID Guide: Find-It-Fast Organic Solutions for Your Garden*. Emmaus, PA: Rodale, 2001 (ISBN 0875968821).

Dirr, Michael. *Dirr's Hardy Trees and Shrubs: An Illustrated Encyclopedia*. Portland, OR: Timber Press, 1997 (ISBN 0881924040).

Ellis, Barbara. *The Organic Gardener's Handbook of Natural Insect and Disease Control: A Complete Problem-Solving Guide to Keeping Your Garden and Yard Healthy Without Chemicals*. Emmaus, PA: Rodale, 1996 (ISBN 0875967531).

———. *Taylor's Weekend Gardening Guide to Easy, Practical Pruning; Techniques for Training Trees, Shrubs, Vines, and Roses*. Boston, MA: Houghton Mifflin, 1997 (ISBN 0395815916).

Gershuny, Grace, ed. *The Rodale Book of Composting: Easy Methods for Every Gardener*. Emmaus, PA: Rodale, 1992 (ISBN 0785579915).

Gilman, Edward F. *Trees for Urban and Suburban Landscape*. Boston, MA: Delmar Publishers, 1997 (ISBN 0827370539).

Greenwood, Pippa. *American Horticultural Society Pests and Diseases: The Complete Guide to Preventing, Identifying and Treating Plant Problems*. New York, NY: DK Adult, 2000 (ISBN 0789450747).

Hill, Lewis. *Pruning Made Easy: A Gardener's Visual Guide to When and How to Prune Everything from Flowers to Trees*. North Adams, MA: Storey Publishing, 1998 (ISBN 1580170064).

Lamott, Anne. *Bird by Bird: Some Instructions on Writing and Life*. Wilmington, NC: Anchor Publishing, 1995 (ISBN 0385480016).

Lancaster, Roy. *The Pruning of Trees, Shrubs and Conifers*. Portland, OR: Timber Press, 2004 (ISBN 0881926132).

Macunovich, Janet, and Steve Nikkla. *Caring for Perennials: What to Do and When to Do It.*

North Adams, MA: Storey Publishing, 1997 (ISBN 0882669575).

Reich, Lee. *The Pruning Book*. Newtown, CT: Taunton Press, 1999 (ISBN 1561583162).

————. *Weedless Gardening*. Woodstock, VT: Workman Press, 2001 (ISBN 0761116966).

WEB SITES

backyardgardener.com

bbg.org (Brooklyn Botanic Garden)

Best-Garden-Care.com

bewatersmart.com

bhg.com (Better Homes and Gardens site)

diynet.com/shrubs_trees

doityourself.com

findarticles.com (index of magazine articles on a vast array of subjects, including gardening)

flower-gardening-made-easy.com

freshflowergarden.com

garden.org (National Gardening Association)

gardencom.com

gardening.about.com

gardenweb.com

grabthebasics.com/gardening

helpfulgardener.com

hgtv.com

homeandfamilynetwork.com/gardening

hortchat.com

hortmag.com (*Horticulture* magazine)

landscaping.about.com

magazine-directory.com/Fine-Gardening (*Fine Gardening* magazine)

markcullen.com (especially for Canadian gardeners)

mtvernon.wsu.edu (complete information on pruning grapes)

mygreathome.com/outdoors

perennials.com

plantideas.com

provenwinners.com

savvygardener.com

the-organic-gardener.com

treesaregood.com/treecare

WEB SITES RELATED TO GARDEN TOOLS

cleanairgardening.com (environmentally friendly lawn and garden supplies)

ehow.com (how-to instructions for working with garden tools)

epinions.com (garden tool reviews and comparison shopping)

gardenartisans.com/tools

gardeners.com (Gardener's Supply)

gardenguides.com

gardenhardware.com

gardenscapetools.com

gardentalk.com

gardentoolsofmaine.com

hidatool.com (handmade Japanese garden tools)

igardenworld.com

lifewithease.com/garden (ergonomically designed garden tools)

nybgshopinthegarden.org (New York Botanic Garden shop)

pbs.org/wgbh/victorygarden/knowhow/tools

porticogreen.web.aplus.net/heirloomtools

realgoods.com

surfnetkids.com/games/garden (garden tools for kids)

SOFTWARE RELATED TO GARDEN MAINTENANCE AND PLANTING

gardenguides.com

gardeninglaunchpad.com

horticopia.com (see especially *Illustrated Pruning and Planting*)

pleasantlakesoftware.com

U.S. REGIONAL GARDENING INFORMATION

REGIONAL WEB-BASED RESEARCH YOU COULD DO

- Google the extension service at a college or university in your state or region. Here are a few: montana.edu; ag.arizona.edu/gardening; umassgreeninfo.org; hgic.clemson.edu; ext.vt.edu; mnlandscaping.org; ext.colostate.edu.
- Google arboretums or botanical gardens in your region, such as mortonarb.org/plant info; huntingtonbotanical.org; chicagobotanic.org; mobot.org.
- Go to local.com, type in your state, then "garden maintenance" for a list of garden maintenance businesses in your area. Go to servicemagic.com for a similar service.

GO TO THESE WEB SITES AND ENTER YOUR REGION

cambiumgardening.com/books/regional-guides

forums.gardenweb.com

gardeninginstitute.com/indexer (Michigan State University site with links to centers for gardening information across the United States)

usna.usda.gov/Gardens/invasives (U.S. National Arboretum site with links to every state, with information by state on invasive plants and a vast range of other regional and state-by-state gardening information)

SPECIFIC REGIONAL INFORMATION

SOUTHEAST

WEB SITES

alibris.com (Southeast gardening books)

carolinagardener.com

leon.ifas.ufl.edu/gardening_landscaping.htm
(University of Florida Web site)

plantdelights.com

southerngardening.com

BOOKS

American Horticultural Society staff. *Southeast: Smart Garden Regional Guide.* New York, NY: DK Books, 2004 (ISBN 0789494949).

Black, Robert, ed. *Your Florida Landscape: A Complete Guide to Planting and Maintenance.* Gainesville, FL: University Press of Florida, 1998 (ISBN 081301641X).

Haehle, Robert G. *Native Florida Plants: Low Maintenance Landscaping and Gardening.* Charlestown, WV: Taylor Books, 2004 (ISBN 1589790510).

Robinson, Olive, et al. *Peachtree Garden Book: Gardening in the Southeast.* Atlanta, GA: Peachtree Publishing, 1997 (ISBN 1561451444).

Rushing, Felder. *Tough Plants for Southern Gar-dens.* Plano, TX: Cool Springs Press, 2003 (ISBN 1591860024).

SOUTHWEST

WEB SITES

ag.Arizona.edu/gardening

cals.arizona.edu/gardening/swsites.html

highplainsgardening.com

johnchapman.com

plantsofthesouthwest.com/plant.html

southwestgardening.com (gardeners' forum)

BOOKS

American Horticultural Society staff. *Southwest: Smart Garden Regional Guide.* New York, NY: DK Books, 2004 (ISBN 0789493675).

Busco, Janice. *First Garden: How to Get Started in Southwest Gardening.* Plano, TX: Thomas Nelson Publishing, 2005 (ISBN 1591861608).

Dolicek, Kelli. *Month-by-Month Gardening in New Mexico.* Austin, TX: Treasure Chest Books, Inc., 1999 (ISBN 1889593028).

Huber, Kathy. *The Texas Flower Garden.* Salt Lake City, UT: Gibbs Smith Publishing, 2005 (ISBN 1586857444).

Phillips, Judith. *New Mexico Gardener's Guide.* Plano, TX: Thomas Nelson Publishing, 2005 (ISBN 1591861179).

Rushing, Felder. *Tough Plants for Texas Gardens.* Plano, TX: Thomas Nelson Publishing, 2005 (ISBN 1591861535).

Sunset editors. *Gardening in the Southwest.* Menlo Park, CA: Sunset Books, 2005 (ISBN 0376037121).

Weinstein, Gail. *All About Dry Climate Gardening.* Des Moines, IA: Meredith Books, 2004 (ISBN 0897214994).

CALIFORNIA

WEB SITES

californiagardens.com

groups.ucanr.org/gardening/ (University of California Cooperative Extension)

sacramentogardening.com

BOOKS

Asakawa, Bruce and Sharon. *California Gardener's Guide.* Plano, TX: Cool Springs Press, 2001 (ISBN 1930604475).

Endicott, Katherine. *Northern California Gardening: A Month-by-Month Guide.* San Francisco, CA: Chronicle Books, 1996 (ISBN 0811809269).

Gilmer, Maureen. *The Complete Guide to Southern California Gardening.* Charleston, WV: Taylor Books, 1995 (ISBN 0878338756).

Holmes, Roger, ed. *Home Landscaping: Califor-

nia Region.* Upper Saddle River, NJ: Creative Homeowner, 2001 (ISBN 1580110460).

Smaus, Bob. *Answers for California Gardeners.* Los Angeles, CA: Los Angeles, CA: Los Angeles Times, 2002 (ISBN 1883792630).

———. *Fifty-Two Weeks in the California Garden.* Los Angeles, CA: Los Angeles Times, 1996 (ISBN 1883792118).

Welsh, Pat. *Pat Welsh's Southern California Gardening: A Month-by-Month Guide.* San Francisco, CA: Chronicle Books, 1999 (ISBN 0811822141).

NORTHWEST

WEB SITES

northwesthort.org

northwestperennialalliance.org

rainyside.com

slugsandsalal.com

BOOKS

American Horticultural Society staff. *Northwest: Successful Plants and Gardening Techniques for Your Area.* New York, NY: DK Books, 2003 (ISBN 0789493667).

Kruckberg, Arthur. *Gardening with Native Plants in the Pacific Northwest.* Seattle, WA: University of Washington Press, 1997 (ISBN 0295974761).

Prinzing, Debra. *Pacific Northwest Garden Survival Guide*. Golden, CO: Fulcrum Publishing, 2004 (ISBN 1555915027).

Stevens, Elaine, et al. *The New Twelve Month Gardener: A West Coast Guide*. Toronto, Ontario, Canada Whitecap Books, 2001 (ISBN 1552850633).

Western

Web Sites

coldclimategardening.com

highcountrygardens.com

Books

Brenzel, Kathleen. *Western Garden Book*. Menlo Park, CA: Sunset Books, 2001 (ISBN 0376038756).

Cretti, John. *Month-by-Month Gardening in the Rocky Mountain*. Plano, TX: Cool Springs Press, 2005 (ISBN 1591860377).

Springer, Lauren, and Scott Proctor. *Passionate Gardening: Good Advice for Challenging Climates*. Golden, CO: Fulcrum Press, 2000 (ISBN 1555913482).

Sunset editors. *Western Garden Book*. Menlo Park, CA: Sunset Books, 1995 (ISBN 0376038519).

————. *Western Garden Problem Solver*. Menlo Park, CA: Sunset Books, 1998 (ISBN 0376061324).

Wann, David. *The Zen of Gardening in the High and Arid West: Tips, Tools, Techniques*. Golden, CO: Fulcrum Press, 2003 (ISBN 1555914578).

Midwest

Web Sites

chicagobotanic.org

midwestgardeningmag.com

midwestliving.com

plant_doctor.typepad.com

Books

Bergmann, Craig. *Sunset Midwestern Landscaping Book*. Menlo Park, CA: Sunset Books, 2001 (ISBN 0376035250).

Duggan, Laara. *The Best Flowers for Midwest Gardens*. Chicago, IL: Chicago Review Press, 1996 (ISBN 1556522603).

Fowler, Veronica. *Gardening in Iowa and Surrounding Area*. Iowa City, IA: University of Iowa Press, 1997 (ISBN 0877455848).

Holmes, Roger. *Home Landscaping: Midwest Region, Including Southern Canada*. Upper Saddle River, NJ: Creative Homeowner, 1999 (ISBN 1580110053).

McKeown, Denny. *Denny McKeown's Complete Guide to Midwest Gardening*. Plano, TX: Taylor Books, 1985 (ISBN 0878333827).

Myers, Melinda. *The Garden Book for Wisconsin. rev. ed.* Plano, TX: Cool Springs Press, 2005 (ISBN 1591860660).

———. *Month-by-Month Gardening in Wisconsin*. Plano, TX: Cool Springs Press, 2001 (ISBN 1888608269).

Porto, Chuck. *Best Garden Plants for Iowa*. Edmonton, Canada: Lone Pine Publishing, 2005 (ISBN 1551055201).

Tyler, Tom. *Indiana Gardener's Guide*. Plano, TX: Cool Springs Press, 1997 (ISBN 1888608404).

NORTHEAST

WEB SITES

forums.gardenweb.com/forums/necoast

newenglandwildflower.org

ppplants.com

thephantomgardener.com/gardenbookshop.html

BOOKS

American Horticultural Society staff. *Northeast: Gardening Techniques for Your Area*. New York, NY: DK Books, 2003 (ISBN 0789494957).

Coleman, Eliot. *The New Organic Grower: A Master Manual of Tools and Techniques for the Home and Market Gardener*. White River Jct., VT: Chelsea Green Publishing, 1995 (ISBN 093003175X).

McDonald, Elvin. *Northeast Gardening*. New York, NY: Macmillan Publishing Co., 1990 (ISBN 0025831259).

Reich, Lee. *A Northeast Gardener's Year*. Boston, MA: Addison Wesley Publishing Co., 1993 (ISBN 0201622335).

Sunset editors. *Sunset's Northeastern Garden*. Menlo Park, CA: Sunset Books, 2001 (ISBN 0376035242).

Index

Page numbers in *italics* refer to illustrations or photographs.

Acer pseudosieboldiana, 57
acidanthera (*Acidanthera*), overwintering of, *187*
Aiken, George, *177*
ajuga, 126
   in winter garden, 161
akebia five-leaf (*Akebia quinata*), 113
allium (*Allium*):
   'Globemaster', 130
   'Hair', 180
   planting bulbs of, 179–81
   seed head interest of, 130–31
Allium aflatunense, 114
   deadheading of, 17, 126
Allium christophii, 130
amsonia (*Amsonia*):
   cutting back of, 161
   hubrechtii, 81
   tabernaemontana, 80, 81
Andros, Howard, 93, 169
anemone, fall-blooming (*Anemone tomentosa*) 'Robustissima', cutting back of, 160–61
annuals, overwintering of, *187*
annuals, planted in pots, 94–99, *95*
   fertilizing of, *96*
   medium for, 94, *95, 96*
   placement of, 94
   plant combinations for, *95*
   selection of, 94–98
   timing of, 94
   watering of, *96*
apple trees, semi-dwarf, 29
apple trees, standard, fruiting and, 29

apple trees, standard, pruning of, 22, 26, *28,* 29–30
   aesthetics of, 26, 29, 30, 31–35
   prunings disposal and, *29,* 30
   purpose of, 29
   sequence of, 30
Aralia racemosa, 81
arbovitae (*Thuja occidentalis*) 'Smaragd', *21,* 22
ash:
   mountain (*Sorbus alnifolia*), 157
   pollarding of, 45
aster, full-blooming, cutting back of, *124,* 161, 168
astilbe, 218
   cutting back of, 161, 168
   deadheading and, 130, 132
aurinia, 57
autumn, garden colors in, *155,* 157
autumn maintenance, 155–214
   checklists for, 50, 204
   work of, 157
axes, sharpening of, 22
azalea, Cornell Pink (*Rhododendron mucronulatum*), 57

backhoes, *72, 74,* 82, 83, 88, 91, *105*
ball carts, 54–57, 94
bamboo stakes, 15, 65, 66
barberry, purple-leaved Japanese (*Berberis thunbergii* 'Atropurpurea'), *114,* 139
bark mulch, processed, 75, 99, 118
   application of, 102–3

bee balm (*Monarda*):
   cutting back of, 158
   'Jacob Cline', 81
beech (*Fagus sylvatica*), training of, 46, *47*
bee sting, remedy for, *148*
beetles, Japanese, 145
Begonia X *tuberhybrida* 'Illumination Apricot', *11*
bergenia, 57
Bird by Bird (Lamott), 17
black haw hedge (*Viburnum prunifolium*), *18*
   trimming of, *146–47*
bleeding heart (*Lamprocapnos spectabilis*), 57
   cutting back of, 158
   'Gold Heart', 81
bleeding heart, everlasting (*Dicentra eximia*), cutting back of, 161
bloodroot (*Sanguinaria canadensis*), 57
   cutting back of, 158
   dividing of, 170, 204
   'Flore Pleno', 169
blueberries, mulching of, 103
body, as most important gardening tool, 173
books, 223–24
boots, muck, 57
botrytis, *93,* 158, 169
boxwood, *24*
   Korean (*Buxus microphylla koreana*), *21*
   trimming of, *147*

brick edging, 151–53
  technique for, 152–53
Brick Wall Garden, 87, *113*
  foliage colors in, *116*
  leaf management in, 192
  renovation of (spring 2005),
    80–81, 91–92
  self-seeding perennials removed
    from, 140
Brown, Richard, 131, 140
brunnera (*Brunnera macrophylla*), 57
  cutting back of, 161
  'Jack Frost', *139,* 140–47
brush piles, building and burning of,
    38–39
buckets, 57
  for weeding, *122*
buckthorn, 139
buckwheat hulls, as mulch, 106
bulb planter, *178, 179,* 180
bulbs:
  hiding foliage of, 179
  ordering of, 143, *183*
  planted in ground, *178,* 179–80,
    181
  planted in pots, 34, 57, 94, 143,
    182–85
burning bush (*Euonymus alatus*)
    'Compactus':
  coppicing of, 42
  as invasive, 139
  pruning of, 41
butterbur (*Petasites japonicus*), 133
butternut, carving sculpture into
    trunk of, 196

Carex buchananii, overwintering of,
    187
catalpa, pollarding of, 45
catmint (*Nepeta* X *faassenii* 'Walker's
    Low'):
  cutting back of, 160
  dividing of, 174
chain saws, 41, 42, 51, 88

checklists:
  for autumn, 50, 204
  for early spring, 107
  for late autumn/early winter, 50
  for late spring, 107–8
  for late winter, 50
  for summer, 149–50
cherry, purple-leaf sand (*Prunus* X
    cistena), 80
cleanup, 24, 54, 59, *69*
  edging, *see* edges, edging
  leaf management, *see* leaf manage-
    ment, spring
cocoa-bean hulls, as mulch, 106
cold cellars, overwintering tulips in,
    34, 57, *185*
coleus, *see Solenostemun* 'Alabama
    Sunset'
Colocasia esculenta 'Illustris', overwin-
    tering of, *187*
columbine, 57
compost, 144
  from autumn raking, 189, 191
  for perennials planting, 92–94, *93*
  for shrub planting, 79, 94
  from spring raking, 63, 65
  technique for, 149
compost piles, 63, 65, 149
  cut-back perennials not added to,
    169
coppicing:
  creation of new, 42
  of deciduous trees, 42–43, 46
  purpose of, 42, 46
  of shrubs, 42–43, 46
  technique for, 42–43
  see also pollarding
Coreopsis verticillata 'Moonbeam',
    deadheading of, 126
Cotinus coggygria 'Royal Purple', 80
crab apple (*Malus*), *54*
  'Adams', 145
  'Donald Wyman', *35, 156*
  'Lollipop', 35

'Prairiefire', *33,* 145
  preventing weeds under, 118
  'Royalty', 145
  selection of, *33, 35,* 145
  'Sugar Tyme', 145
  'Tina', 35
crab apples, pruning of, 22, *31, 32,
    33*
  aesthetics of, 26, 31–35
  sequence of, 31–35
Crambe cordifolia, 16
  cutting back of, 160
  deadheading of, 126
  staking of, 123
crocus, 57

daffodil, *53, 54,* 57, 59, 61
  planting of, 179–80
dame's rocket (*Hesperis matronalis*),
    deadheading of, 126
daylily (*Hemerocallis*), 61, *113,* 219
  cutting back of, 160, 168
  deadheading of, 126, 131–32
  dividing of, 170, 179
  'Happy Returns', deadheading of,
    126
  'Stella d'Oro', deadheading of,
    126
deadheading, *see* perennials, dead-
    heading of
Derreen (garden), 18
Dicentra spectabilis, see bleeding heart
    (*Lamprocapnos spectabilis*)
digitalis:
  cutting back of, 160
  deadheading of, 126
Dig Safe, 88–90
dogwood (*Cornus sanquinea* 'Winter
    Flame'), *105,* 157
dogwood, red-twig dogwood (*Cornus
    alba* 'Elegantissima'):
  coppicing of, 42
  pruning of, 40
dogwood, yellow-twig:

coppicing of, 42
cutting back of, 160
pruning of, 40
drains, curtain, 222
drip lines, house, gardens and,
217–22, *218, 221*
Dry Stone Wallers Association, 199

Echinacea:
cutting back of, 160
purpurea 'Mango Meadowbrite',
81
echinops, deadheading of, 126
edges, edging, 57, 65–69
dropped lawn, *see* lawn edges,
dropped
laying of stone or brick, 151–53
mowing around, 65
edging shears, 68
elderberry, 81
Entry Garden, *54,* 81, *94*
epimedium, 218
cutting back of, 161, 169
Eupatorium rugosum 'Chocolate', 161
euphorbia, cutting back of, 161
evergreens, pine needle mulch for,
103

false cypress (*Chamaecyparis pisifera*)
'Filifera', 22
fern, 218
Christmas, in winter garden, 161
hay-scented (*Dennstaedtia punctilobula*), removal from garden
of, *139,* 140–47, *141,* 204
Japanese painted (*Athyrium nipponicum* 'Pictum'), *141,* 147
maidenhair, cutting back of, 169
fertilizer:
for annuals grown in pots, *96*
see also soil amendments
feverfew (*Matricaria*):
cutting back of, 160
deadheading of, 126, 132

fieldstone, for edging, 152
filbert (*Corylus*), 145
file, diamond dust, *23*
foamflower (*Tiarella cordifolia*), 57
cutting back of, *166*
forsythia, 57
coppicing of, 42
freestanding wall:
definition of, 199
laying stone for, *201*
see also stone walls, dry, repairing
break in

gang Locke lawn mower, 128–29
garages, overwintering bulbs in, 34
garden design:
revising of, *see* lawn shape, changing of for winter beauty, 22
garden help, hiring of, 215–16
gardening, as public act, 15
garden maintenance:
choosing plants for reducing of,
145
definition of, 11
lessons of, 11–12
as management, 16–17
mindfulness and, 12
techniques for reducing of,
144–45
tone, mood, design and, 15–16
work of, 12, 17
Garlick, Robin, 12, 147, 191, 192
gas plant (*Dictamnus albus*), 135
cutting back of, 130, 161
geranium, hardy (*Geranium*), 81,
113
bigroot (*macrorrhizum*), 161
bigroot (*macrorrhizum*), 'Ingwersen's Variety', 174
cutting back of, *124,* 161
deadheading of, 126
dividing of, 174
oxonianum 'Claridge Druce',
124

as weed deterrents, 118
geum, 126
Gillman, Ed, 71
ginger, European (*Asarum
europaeum*), in winter garden,
161
glasses, safety, 173
gloves, 173
goatskin, *21,* 57
rubber-palmed, 57
goatsbeard (*Aruncus dioicus*), 81, 126
Godwin, Will and Sara Anne, garden
of, 15
gooseberries, mulching of, 103
gooseneck loosetrife (*Lysimachia
clethroides*), 133
Gordon, Peter, 29
grapevines, pruning of, 35–36
grasses, ornamental, *24*
dividing of, 170–72, *171,* 177
dried and displayed in pots, *162,
163, 164,* 204
fountain (*Pennisetum setaceum*),
51, 204
giant miscanthus (*Miscanthus
floridulus*), confining growth
of, 133
invasive, 133
maiden, 51
managing and cutting back of, 51,
59, *162, 163, 164*
purple-reed, *see* purple-reed grass
(*Miscanthus sinensis*) 'Purpurascens'
ribbon (*Phalaris arundinacea
'Picta'*), 133
staking of, 123
in winter garden, *24,* 161, *167*
Gray Garden, 81
Green Mountain Glove Company,
21, 57
ground covers:
house drip lines and plantings of,
218–19

ground covers (*continued*)
  used as weed deterrents, 118

hammers, mash, 173
hats, 57
hay, baled, as mulch, 103–6
Hayward, Gordon, 217–22
  farm upbringing and work ethic
    of, 12, 14, 22, 29
  lawn mowing duties of, 117,
    128–29
Hayward, Mary:
  farm upbringing of, 12, 14
  garden walks of Gordon and,
    113–15
  weeding tasks of, 12, 117,
    118–23, *122, 124,* 131, 134,
    136, 141, 147
Heath, Brent and Becky, ordering
  bulbs from, 143, *183*
hedges, replacing old shrubs with,
  82–87, *85, 86*
hedges, trimming of, 147–49
  technique for, *146,* 149
  timing of, 149
  tools for, *146,* 149
hedge shears, 124
  sharpening of, 22
helenium (*Helenium*):
  cutting back of, 160, 168
  'Moerheim Beauty', *113*
  'Riverton Beauty', cutting back of,
    161
helianthus, cutting back of, 158, 168
Heliopsis helianthoides 'Summer Sun',
  uprooting of, 204
Herb Garden, *53*
  lawn vs. pea-stone paths in, 122
herbs, annual, covering pots of, 204
heuchera, 80–81
  cutting back of, 161
  deadheading of, 126
Hibiscus acetosella 'Maple Sugar', *99*
hoes:

hand, 57, 122
  scuffle, *118,* 120
  sharpening of, 22
hollyhock:
  cutting back of, 158–60, 169
  deadheading of, 126
  staking of, *123*
Holway, Alice, 177
honeysuckle, 139
hosta (*Hosta*), 218
  cutting back of, 160, 161, *167,*
    168
  'Royal Standard', *117*
  'Sagae', 80–81
  'Sum and Substance', deadheading
    of, 133
Hunt, Greg, 105
Hydrangea paniculata, 82
  'White Dome', 81, 91–92
Hylotelephium spectabile:
  'Autumn Joy', in winter garden,
    161
  ornamental seed heads of, 126,
    131, 204

Intimate Garden, The (Hayward and
  Hayward), 16
invasive plants:
  aggressive seeds and roots of, 126,
    132, 140, 145, 204
  confinement of, 133
  environmental imbalance created
    by, 139
  removing of, 139–47, *141, 143*
iris, bearded (*Iris germanica*):
  deadheading of, 126, 132
  in winter garden, 161, *168*
iris, Siberian (*Iris sibirica*), 219
  cutting back of, 161, 168
  deadheading of, 126, 135
  dividing of, 179

Joe Pye weed (*Eupatorium maculatum*):

'Gateway', 123, *162*
  reducing size of, 204

Katsura tree, *192*
Kirengeshoma palmata, cutting back
  of, 161
kitchen knife, serrated, *160,* 168
kneeing pads, *117,* 120, 122, 135,
  136
knotweed, Japanese, 139
kudzu vine, 139

ladders:
  apple-picking, 29–30
  for hedge trimming, 147, 149
lady's mantle (*Alchemilla mollis*), 80
  deadheading of, 126
  self-seeding aggressiveness of, 140,
    204
lamb's ears (*Stachys byzantina*), cutting back of, 161
lamium, cutting back of, 161
Lamott, Anne, 17
landscape fabric:
  for backfilling retaining walls, 203
  on pea-stone paths, *118,* 120
Larsen, Torben, *72, 74, 75,* 82, 83,
    88, 91, *105,* 111
lawn clippings, as mulch, 99, 106
lawn edges, dropped, 57
  maintenance of, 68
  purpose of, 65
  soil and, 67–68
  steps in creation of, 65–69
  time spent on, 65
  tools and equipment for, 65–66
lawn mowers:
  gang Locke lawn mower, 128–29
  lawn tractors, *see* lawn tractors
lawn paths, pea-stone vs., *118,* 122,
    145
lawn roller, 110
lawns:
  spring raking of, 59

234 ■

see also edges, edging; lawn edges, dropped; mowing; sod, sod lawn

lawn shaping, changing of, 205–12, *208, 209, 210, 211*
   garden area transitions in, 207–12
   purpose of, 205
   relating previously unrelated bed, 207
   tool for, 205, 212
   tree drip lines as edges in, 205–6
   using nearby features as cues in, 206

lawn tractor, *105,* 128–29
   leaf mulcher attachment on, *60, 64–65, 188, 189,* 191
   taking care of, 128

leaf blowers, gas-powered, 190, 191–92

leaf management, autumn, 157, *188,* 189–92
   cutting back perennials in, 157
   easier spring cleanup dependent on, 61
   rakes vs. leaf blowers in, 191–92
   see also raking, autumn

leaf management, spring, 59–64
   dependent on autumn cleanup, 61
   with lawn tractor and mulcher attachment, *60,* 64–65
   removal by hand, *63,* 64
   see also raking, spring

leaf mold, 75, *143,* 144
   formation of, 103, 189
   for perennials plantings, 92, *93,* 103, 118

Leucanthemum superbum 'Becky':
   cutting back of, 160, 169
   deadheading of, 126

ligularia:
   cutting back of, *158*
   deadheading of, 126
   dentata 'Britt-Marie Crawford', 81

lilac (*Syringa* spp.):

fertilizing of, 39
late (*Syringa villosa*), removal of, 87–91
   pruning of, 40
tree (*Syringa reticulata*), 82
   vulgaris 'Sensation', 82

lilac hedge, digging up and replacing of, 82–87, *85, 86*
lily-of-the-valley, weeding of, 123
lily-of-the-valley shrub (*Pieris japonica*), 57
   pruning of, 40
linden, pollarding of, 45

Lobelia cardinalis:
   cutting back of, 160
   self-seeding aggressiveness of, 140, 160

Lobelia siphilitica, 80, 108, 140
   'Alba', 80
   cutting back of, 160
   deadheading of, 126, 145

locust, black, used as vine support, 196

Long Borders, *24, 114*
   cutting back of, *162, 165*

lopping, shears, 40
   sharpening of, 22, *23*

MacFarland, Siena, 12, 61, 147
magnolia, 57
mallow, deadheading of, 126
manure, composted, 144
   for perennials planting, 92, *93*
maple, English hedge (*Acer campestre*), 146
masterwort (*Astrantia major*):
   deadheading of, 132
   'Rosea', uprooting of, 204
Maurice, Dymock, 41, 81
mint, 133
mockorange (*Philadelphus coronarius*), pruning of, 40
Mondon, Eva, 115
mountain laurel (*Kalmia latifolia*),

pruning of, 40
mowing, 12, 128–29
   in autumn, 157
   around edging, 65
   of sod lawn, 111
   techniques for, 128
   see also lawn tractors

mulches, mulching, 99–106
   application of, 99–102
   organic, 99
   purpose of, 99, 118, 145
   after removal of invasive plants, *143*
   timing of, 99–102
   and tree planting, *75*
   types of, 99, 102–6
   whole-leaf, 103
   volcano, 103
   wood-based, 103

nepeta, deadheading of, 126
Nicotiana 'Fragrant Cloud', *113*
ninebark, common (*Physocarpus opulifolius*):
   'Dart's Gold', 83
   'Diabolo', *114,* 139
nursery, delivery from, 104–5

oak, pollarding of, 45
obedient plant (*Physostegia virginiana*), 133
Onza (cat), *34*
Osmacote, *96*

paths, pea-stone, 145
   installing of, 120
   lawn paths vs., *118,* 122, 145
   maintenance of, *118,* 120–22
Patten Seed Company, Web site of, 109
paving materials, for reduced maintenance, 144–45
pea shrub, weeping (*Caragana arborescens*) 'Pendula', *21*

peony (*Paeonia*), 61
    'Claudia', *113*
    cutting back of, 130, 158, *159*
    deadheading and, 130
    dividing of, 177, 204
    planting of, *93*
    'Roselette', 114
    staking of, 123
perennial bed maintenance:
    cutting back of plants in, *124*
    edging between lawn and, 57,
        65–69, 151
    staking, 123–25
    top dressing, 157
    weeding, 12, 54, 117–23
perennials:
    and Brick Walk Garden renova-
        tion, 80–81
    as cover for ripening bulb foliage,
        179
    dried, for winter bouquets, 204
    invasive, *see* invasive plants
    leaving seed heads on, 130–31,
        145
    massed, as weed deterrents, 118
    mulching of, 103
    planting of, 92–94, *93*
    raking around, 61, *63*
    reducing size of, 204
    in winter garden, 161
perennials, cutting back of, 157–69,
        158, 159, 160, 162, 164, 165,
        166, 167, 168
    in early to mid-October, 160
    in mid- to late October, 160–61
    in mid- to late September, 158–60
    purpose of, 157, 158–60
    in spring, 157
    in summer, 124
    techniques for, 168–69
perennials, deadheading of, 125–36
    reasons for, 125, 126–30, 145
    and when to leave plants intact,
        130–31, 145

see also specific perennials
perennials, dividing of, 169–79, *170,*
        171, 172, 174, 175, 204
    cutmint and other smaller peren-
        nials, 174
    daylily, 170, 179
    ornamental grasses, 170–72, *171,*
        177
    peony, 177, 204
    potential growth from, 169
    purpose of, 177
Perilla, 113
periwinkle (*Vinca minor*) 'Bowles',
        57, 218–19
pH:
    testing of, 110
    of topsoil, 144, 214
phlox, woodland (*Phlox divaricata*),
        54, 57
    cutting back in autumn of, 16–17,
        166, 168–69
    cutting back in summer of, *124*
Phlox paniculata, cutting back of,
        158
Phlox stolonifera, 57, 192
    cutting back of, *166,* 168
pine, dwarf Scots (*Pinus sylvestris*)
        'Nana', 22
pine boughs, as perennials mulch,
        103
pine needles, as mulch, 99, 103
plantain weed, as bee sting remedy,
        148
pollarding, 43–46
    purpose of, 46
    technique of, 45
    trees for, 45, 46
    see also coppicing
Potentilla fruticosa, 82
pots:
    annuals planted in, *see* annuals
        planted in pots
    herbs in, 204
    and reduced maintenance, 145

tulips planted in, 34, 57, 94, 143,
        182–85
poppy:
    Oriental, in winter garden, 161
    plume (*Macleaya cordata*), 133
powdery mildew, 158
primula, 57
    Candelabra (*Primula japonica*),
        deadheading of, 126, 133–34,
        145
Pro-Mix, 94, *95, 96*
Prozzo, Gerry, 196
pruning:
    coppicing, *see* coppicing
    of crab apple, *see* crab apple, prun-
        ing of
    of deciduous trees, *see* trees (decid-
        uous), pruning of
    of grapevines, 35–36
    of native trees, 196–97
    of ornamental grasses, 51
    pleasures of, 12
    pollarding, *see* pollarding
    of shrubs, *see* shrubs, pruning of
    of standard apple trees, *see* apple
        trees, standard, pruning of
    of trumpet vine (*Campsis radi-*
        cans), 38
    tying up vs., *37*
pruning saws, 25, *26,* 40
pruning shears:
    bypass vs. anvil, 23
    Felco, *23,* 57
    sharpening of, 22, *23,* 136
pry bars, 173
pulmonaria, 57
    cutting back of, 161
    self-seeding aggressiveness of, 140
purple-reed grass (*Miscanthus*
        sinensis) 'Purpurascens', 80,
        113
    dividing of, 177
    managing and cutting back of, 51
    in winter garden, *24,* 161, *162*

purple-reed grass (*Miscanthus sinensis*) 'Variegatus', dividing of, 170–72, *171*
Putney Nursery, 177

rakes, raking:
    directly onto tarps, *60,* 61, 192
    flipping vs. dragging in, *58,* 61
    types of, 61–63
raking, autumn, 157, 189, 191–92
    compost from, 189, 191
    winds and, 189, 191
raking, spring, 59–64
    of perennial beds, 61, *63*
    purpose of, 59–61, *62*
    stages in, 63–64
    timing of, 61
    winds and, 61, 63, 64
Ranney, Philip, *155*
raspberries, mulching of, *103,* 106
regional gardening information, U.S., 225–29
retaining wall, 200
    backfilling of, 203
    definition of, 199
    key to longevity of, *198*
    see also stone walls, dry, repairing break in
rhododendron:
    mulch as weed deterrence under, 118
    pruning of, 40
rock garden, leaf management in, 191–92
Rodgersia pinnata, 81
Rosa glauca, 80, *113*
Rubus cockburnianus, 81
Rudbeckia fulgida 'Goldsturm', not cut back, 131, 161
Russian sage (*Perovskia atriplicifolia*), 59, 107
    not cut back in autumn, 161
rust, 160, 169

Sales, John, 16
Sanzone, Patricia, 12, 61, 68, 147, *148*
Savery, Tom, Prison Garden of, 133
sawdust, 103
saws:
    chain, 41, 42, 51, 91
    pruning, 25, *26,* 40
Schoenemann, Oscar, Locke lawn mower of, 128–29
Scotch thistle, deadheading of, 126
scratcher, three-pronged, 120
scuffle hoe, *118,* 120
sealing compound, *26*
Sedum spectabile, see Hylotelephium spectabile
seeds, seeding:
    self-, 126, 132, 140, 145, 204
    sodding vs., 109
shadblow (*Amelanchier* X *grandiflora*) 'Autumn Brilliance', 71, *105*
Shasta daisies, 219
shovels, sharpening of, 22
shrubs:
    assessing of, 87, 91–92
    and Brick Walk Garden renovation, 80, 81, 91–92
    multistemmed, 40
    old, removing of, 87–91
    raking around, 61
    that bloom on new wood, 219
    transplanting of, 91–92, 145
shrubs, container-grown, planting of, 77–82
    backfill for, 79
    hole after, 79
    root-bound, 79–82
shrubs, planting of, 77–87
    balled-and-burlapped, 77
    replacing old shrubs with new hedge, 82–87, *85, 86*
shrubs, pruning of, 40–43, *41*
    coppicing and, 42–43, 46
    with flexible branches, 219

with prostrate growth habit, 219
    single-stemmed with many branches, 40
slugs, 160
snakeroot, purple-leaved (*Actaea simplex* 'Brunette'), *162*
Snow, Dan, 158, 173, 198–99, 200, 202
snowdrops, dividing of, 100–101
sod, sod lawn:
    laying of, 110
    leftover, using of, 108
    maintaining of, 111
    measuring for, 109
    seeding vs., 109
soil:
    compaction of, 24, 53
    and dropped lawn edging, 67–68
    preparation of, for perennial planting, 92–94
    testing of, 110, 144
    see also topsoil
soil amendments, 144
    for perennials planting, 92–94, *93*
    for shrub planting, 79, 94
    tree planting and, 71, 94
soilless medium, for growing tulips in pots, 94, *95, 96, 182*
Solenostemun 'Alabama Sunset', *99*
Solomon's seal, (*Polygonatum odoratum*) 'Variegatum', cutting back of, 161
spade, straight-nosed, 65–66, 122, 170, 205
    evaluation of, 66
    lawn shape revised with, 205, 206, 212
spading forks, 170, *171,* 172
spring maintenance, 24, 53–112
    checklists for, 106–8
    earliest chores of, 24, 53–57, 59
spruce, Colorado (*Picea pungens*) 'Glauca Fastigiata', *37*

staking:
    and garden tone, 15–16
    with homemade supports, 125
    of perennials, 123–25
stepping-stones, weeding between,
    121, 122–23
stone cut, for edging, 151–52
stone edging, laying of, 151–53
stone walls, dry:
    tools for building of, 173
    types of, 199
stone walls, dry, repairing break in,
    198–203
    backfilling in, 203
    batter in, 202
    bedding in, 202
    capping in, 203
    choosing where to begin in,
      200
    goal in, 199
    handling stone for, 199–200
    hearting in, 200, 202
    joints in, 202
    laying stones in, 200, *201*
    reasons for, 199
    satisfaction in, 198, 203
    through stones in, 203
straw, baled, as mulch, 103–6
strawberries, mulching for, 106
string-trimmers, string-trimming:
    lawn edge clipping by, 68
    of perennials, 16–17, *166,* 169
Sturdza, Princess Greta, 135–36
sumac, coppicing of, 42
summer maintenance, 113–54
    checklists for, 149–50
sweet cicely, 126
sycamore (*Platanus* X *acerifolia*)
    'Bloodgood', pollarding of,
    45–46

tarpaulin, 48–49, 57
    for cutting back of perennials, 49,
    162, 165

for hedge trimming, *146,* 147,
    149
    other uses for, 49, *159*
    raking directly onto, *60,* 61, 192
    for tree pruning collection, *29,* 30
    types and sizes of, 49
    weeding and, 48
teasel, deadheading of, 126
Tending Your Garden (Hayward and
    Hayward), purpose of, 14–15
Thalictrum rochebrunianum, cutting
    back of, 161
Thoreau, Henry David, 117, 140
tools:
    body as, 173
    for building stone walls, 173
    for dividing perennials, 170, *171,*
      172
    for dropped lawn edging, 65–66
    for hedge trimming, *146,* 149
    necessary, 57
    for planting bulbs, *178,* 179–80
    sharpening of, 22, *23*
    for weeding, *117, 118,* 120, 122,
      122, 123, 135, *136, 141,* 147
    see also specific tools
tools sheds, *16*
topsoil:
    checking source of, 144, 213
    checking structure and texture of,
      213–14
    organic matter in, 214
    pH of, 214
    purchasing of, 213–14
    receiving delivery and storing of,
      214
    salts in, 214
tradescantia, 80
training, of trees and shrubs, 46, *47*
trees:
    autumn assessment of, 196–97
    evergreen, tying up vs. pruning
      branches of, *37*
    in garden centers, selection of, 76

training of, 46, *47*
trees, planting of:
    hole for, 71, *72, 73, 74*
    minding tree roots in, 71
    mulching and, *75*
    new vs. old techniques in, 71
    positioning root ball in, *72*
    removing burlap and wire basket
      in, *72,* 77, *105*
    sequence of, 71–72
    soil amendments and, 71, 94
    staking and, 77
    watering and, *75*
trees (deciduous), pruning of, 25–35
    and autumn assessment, 196–97
    coppicing of, 42–43
    crab apple trees, *see* crab apple
      trees, pruning of
    standard apple, *see* apple trees,
      standard, pruning of
    high, 196, 197
    sequence for, *25–26*
tree trunks:
    carvings in, 196
    left after cutting as vine support,
      196
trumpet vine (*Campsis radicans*),
    pruning of, 38
tulip (*Tulipa*):
    'Blushing Lady', *184*
    'Garant', *184*
    'Gudoshnik', *184*
    planted in pots, 34, *54,* 57, 94,
      143, *182–85*
turtlehead (*Chelone lyonii*), cutting
    back of, 160
twine, 65, 66

utility lines, underground, 88–90

Vasterival (garden), deadheading at,
    135–36
vegetables, mulching for, 106
verbascum, cutting back of, 160, 169

viola, 57, 80
Virginia bluebells (*Mertensia virginica*), *53,* 54
Vitzthum, Quita, 135
volcano mulching, 103

Waldsteinia ternata, not cut back in autumn, 161
walls, dry stone, *see* stone walls, dry
Ward, Jacky, 18
water sprouts, pruning of, 30, *31, 32*
wayfaring tree (*Viburnum lantana* 'Mohican'), coppicing of, 42
Web sites, 224–25, 226, 227, 228, 229
weeds, weeding, 12, 54, 117–23
    Mary Hayward's rules for, 118–20, 144
    on pea-stone paths, *118,* 120–22

prevention of, 117–18
    to reduce maintenance, 144
    between stepping-stones, *121,* 122–23
    tools for, 48, *117, 118,* 120, 122, *122,* 123, 135, *136, 141,* 147
wheelbarrows:
    Dutch, 57
    for weeding and deadheading, 122, 135, 136
wild oats (*Uvularia grandiflora*), 57
willows, pollarding of, 43–45, *113*
winter:
    benefits of, 21, 22–24, 53
    garden beauty and rewards in, 22, 155–57
    gardening impatience in, 24, 53
winter maintenance, 21–52
    checklists for, 50

Wisteria 'Aunt Dee', 196
witch hazel, mulch as weed deterrence under, 118
Woodland Garden, 81, 87, 91–92, 102–3
    cutting back perennials in, *166*
    leaf management in, 192
    plants in, *53,* 54, 57
    spreading woodland phlox in, 16–17

yellowwood, 157
    pruning of, *25–26*
yew (*Taxus* X *media* 'Hicksii'), as hedges, *18,* 82–87, *83, 84, 85, 86,* 91, *105,* 155–56
Your House, Your Garden (Hayward), 217–22